ENGLISH G

6

LIGHTHOUSE

Wordmaster

Cornelsen

Hello and welcome!

*Vor dir liegt der **Wordmaster**. Er hilft dir beim Wörterlernen.*

*Im Anschluss an die **New words** gibt es kurze Aufgaben, Rätsel und Wortspiele, mit denen du den neuen Wortschatz übst und festigst.*

*Sobald du neue Wörter in der Schule besprochen hast, bearbeite die **New words** in diesem Heft.*

*Die **fett gedruckten** deutschen Wörter sind Lernwörter. Sie fehlen im englischen Satz, damit du sie eintragen kannst.*

Alle Lösungen findest du in der Mitte des Heftes.

Embrace diversity

New words ▸ p. 10 | VOCABULARY p. 210

1 Ich bin so glücklich! Ich könnte die ganze Welt **umarmen**.	I'm so happy! I could ______________ the whole world.
2 Berlin ist bekannt für die **Vielfalt** seiner Bewohner.	Berlin is known for the ______________ of its citizens.
3 Südafrika ist eine **multikulturelle** Gesellschaft.	South Africa is a ______________ society.
4 Wenn es im Sommer regnet, sieht man oft **Regenbögen**.	When it rains in summer you can often see ______________.
5 Auch die Deutschen **kolonisierten** Afrika.	The Germans ______________ Africa too.
6 **Diamanten** sind sehr teuer.	______________ are very expensive.
7 Wir hatten eine **Mischung** aus Sonne und Regen im Urlaub.	We had a ______________ of sunshine and rain on our holiday.
8 Es gibt viele verschiedene **Religionen** auf der Welt.	There are many different ______________ around the world.
9 Jana liebt **farbenfrohe** Kleider.	Jana loves ______________ dresses.
10 Afrikas **Tierwelt** ist faszinierend.	Africa's ______________ is fascinating.
11 Im Januar haben wir hier sehr **niedrige** Temperaturen.	Temperatures in January are very ______________ here.
12 Welche **Währung** benutzt man in Südafrika?	What ______________ do they use in South Africa?

1 Find the right words

Finde zu jedem Nomen das passende Adjektiv und übersetze alle Wörter ins Deutsche.

1 diversity ______________ ______________ ______________

2 culture ______________ ______________ ______________

3 religion ______________ ______________ ______________

New words ▸ *p. 11 | VOCABULARY p. 210*

1 Die Rassentrennung in Südafrika wird **Apartheid** genannt.	Race segregation in South Africa is called ______________.
2 Die Südafrikaner **wurden** bis 1994 nach ihrer Hautfarbe **getrennt**.	South Africans ______________ according to their skin colour until 1994.
3 Wir haben kein **öffentliches** Schwimmbad im Ort.	Our town doesn't have a ______________ swimming pool.
4 Was hältst du von unserem Bildungs**system**?	What do you think about our educational ______________?
5 Ich **wurde** gestern aus dem Krankenhaus **entlassen**.	I ______________ from hospital yesterday.
6 Mein Freund ist **mehrsprachig**. Er spricht Deutsch, Englisch und Türkisch.	My friend is ______________. He speaks German, English and Turkish.

2 Find the right words

Finde zu jedem Nomen das passende Verb und übersetze alle Wörter ins Deutsche.

1 colony ______________ ______________ ______________

2 segregation ______________ ______________ ______________

3 release ______________ ______________ ______________

3 Lost words

Setze die Wörter aus den Seifenblasen ein.

1 He was released ______________ prison.

2 They always play an interesting mix ______________ music.

3 Winter ______________ South Africa is ______________ May and August.

4 Mariama speaks English and Zulu ______________ home.

5 A lot of people protested ______________ apartheid.

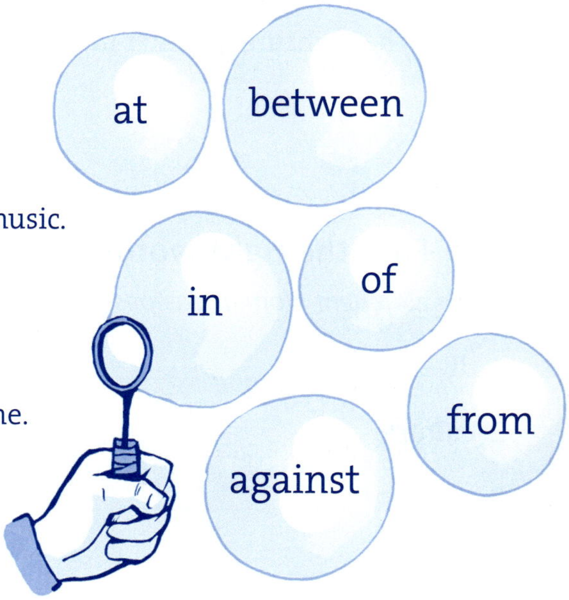

New words ▸ *pp. 12 – 13 | VOCABULARY pp. 211 – 212*

1 Meine Kindheit war anders als deine, weil es **damals** kein Internet gab.	My childhood was different from yours because there was no internet ______________.
2 Sie **wählten** sie zur Präsidentin.	They ________________ her ________ president.
3 Ich habe keine **Erinnerung an** meine ersten drei Lebensjahre.	I have no ________________________________ the first three years of my life.
4 Viele Afrikaner haben keinen **Zugang** zu sauberem Wasser.	Lots of Africans have no ____________________ to clean water.
5 Sie leben in extremer **Armut**.	They live in extreme ______________________.
6 **Arbeitslosigkeit** verursacht große Probleme.	__________________________________ causes big problems.
7 Wir wohnen in einem **Vorort** von Berlin.	We live in a ______________________ of Berlin.
8 **Bäcker** müssen sehr früh aufstehen.	____________________________ have to get up very early.
9 Sie hat ein gutes **Verhältnis** zu ihrer Schwester.	She has a good ___________________________ with her sister.
10 Ich war **total** geschockt, als ich sah, dass jemand in meine Wohnung eingebrochen war.	I was ______________________ shocked when I saw that someone had broken into my flat.
11 Ich **bin** fünf Jahre mit Tom **gegangen**.	I _______________________ Tom for five years.
12 Ich hatte nie die **Möglichkeit**, im Ausland zu studieren.	I never had the ___________________________ to study abroad.
13 Die Polizei **dokumentierte** den Unfall.	The police ____________________ the accident.
14 Ich weiß nichts über das **politische** System in Südafrika.	I don't know anything about South Africa's _________________________________ system.
15 Der 3. Oktober ist Deutschlands **Nationalfeiertag**.	The 3rd October is Germany's ________________ ______________________.

4 What's the word: *chance, opportunity, possibility* or *way*?

Füge das richtige Wort in die Sätze ein.

1 I never had the ________________ to study abroad.

2 Is there a ________________ of meeting your parents when we're in Berlin?

3 There are two ________________ to get to the city centre: you can walk or take the bus.

4 We won't get another ________________ to go to Australia – so let's go this year!

New words ▸ *p. 14 | VOCABULARY p. 212*

1 Ich habe noch nie Elefanten **in freier Wildbahn** gesehen.	I've never seen elephants ________________ .
2 Sie ist **trotz** ihrer Behinderung sehr fit.	She is very fit ________________ her disability.
3 Dies ist die **einmalige** Gelegenheit, im Ausland zu arbeiten.	This is a ________________ opportunity to work abroad.
4 Ich habe gestern einen sehr **informativen** Vortrag über Spinnen gehört.	I listened to a very ________________ talk on spiders yesterday.
5 Die Regierung sollte mehr Geld für den **Naturschutz** ausgeben.	The government should spend more money on ________________ .
6 **Tritt** mir bitte nicht auf den Fuß.	Please don't ________________ on my foot.
7 Komm von der **Kante** weg.	Come away from the ________________ .
8 Der Zug fährt von **Gleis** 3.	The train goes from ________________ 3.
9 Der **Strauß** ist ein großer Vogel, der in Afrika lebt.	The ________________ is a big bird that lives in Africa.
10 Es tut mir **wirklich** leid, wenn ich dich verletzt habe.	I'm ________________ sorry if I hurt you.
11 Unser Baby **wiegt** jetzt 6 Kilo.	Our baby now ________________ 6 kilos.
12 An wen **richtet** sich die Anzeige?	Who is this advert ________________ at?
13 Kennst du **wirksame** Maßnahmen gegen Ratten?	Do you know any ________________ steps against rats?

New words ▸ *p. 15 | VOCABULARY pp. 212–213*

1 Ich mache lieber Sport **anstatt** zu Hause herumzusitzen.	I like doing sports ______________ sitting at home.
2 Vielen Dank im **Voraus**!	Thank you in ______________.
3 Ich habe sie mehrmals angeschrieben, aber ich habe keine **Antwort** bekommen.	I wrote to her a few times, but I got no ______________.
4 Alles ist **besser** als tatenlos herumzusitzen.	Anything is ______________ to sitting around doing nothing.
5 Wenn du bei einer Gastfamilie wohnst, bekommst du einen besseren **Einblick** in das Land.	When you live with a host family, you get a better ______________ into the country.
6 Die Pflanze ist für **Menschen** und Tiere gefährlich.	The plant is dangerous for ______________ and animals.
7 Sie sah aus wie ein **Geschöpf** von einem anderen Planeten.	She looked like a ______________ from another planet.

5 What are the words?

Trage die englischen Wörter in das Kammrätsel ein.
Wie lautet das Lösungswort?

① 

⑤ 

3 a band of different colours that you can see in the sky when the sun shines through rain
6 opposite of "private"
7 a more formal word for "answer"

④ 

② 

Lösungswort: ______________________

6 How do you say the words?

Sieh dir die Wörter auf dem Zettel an und überlege, auf welcher Silbe du sie betonen musst. Ordne sie den richtigen Töpfen zu.

creature
diamond
diversity
document
effective
informative
political – public
relationship
system

New words ▸ *p. 16 | VOCABULARY p. 213*

1 Ich hätte gern Kartoffeln **anstatt** Reis.	I'd like potatoes ____________ rice.
2 Du siehst **verwirrt** aus. Kann ich dir helfen?	You're looking ____________. Can I help you?
3 Ich weiß nicht, wann er kommt. **Eigentlich** weiß ich nicht, ob er überhaupt kommt.	I don't know when he is coming. ____________, I don't know if he's coming at all.
4 Die **Mehrheit** meiner Freunde wohnt in Berlin.	The ____________ of my friends live in Berlin.
5 Unsere Firma wurde Anfang des 20. **Jahrhunderts** gegründet.	Our company was founded at the beginning of the 20th ____________.
6 Englisch dient oft als **Lingua Franca**.	English is often used as a ____________.

7 What's the right word?

Unterstreiche das Wort, das in den Satz passt.

1 The South African currency / system / religion is the rand.
2 Nelson Mandela was segregated / elected / released from prison in 1990.
3 He had fought against apartheid / appartheid / apartheit for many years.
4 He went to prison rather / rather than / than rather give up his fight.
5 The film gives an insight / insite / inside into life in South Africa.
6 Waiting inside is preferably / preferred / preferable to standing in the cold.

New words ▸ *pp. 17–18 | VOCABULARY pp. 213–214*

1 Terrorismus ist zu einer **permanenten** Gefahr in Europa geworden.	Terrorism has become a ____________ danger in Europe.
2 Am Ende einer Frage musst du ein **Fragezeichen** setzen.	You have to put a ____________ at the end of a question.
3 Schlüssel verloren? Das ist **typisch für** dich!	Lost your key? That's ____________ you.
4 Wörter, die im Deutschen und Englischen ähnlich aussehen, aber Unterschiedliches meinen, werden **„falsche Freunde"** genannt.	Words that look similar in German and English but have different meanings are called ____________.

8 What's the right word?

Setze das richtige Wort in die Sätze ein.

1 I ____________ walking ____________ cycling.

2 Can I have potatoes ____________ rice, please?

3 We'd like to move north again, ____________ to Kiel.

4 If I you don't like meat, you can have fish ____________.

5 I think fruit is ____________ chocolate.

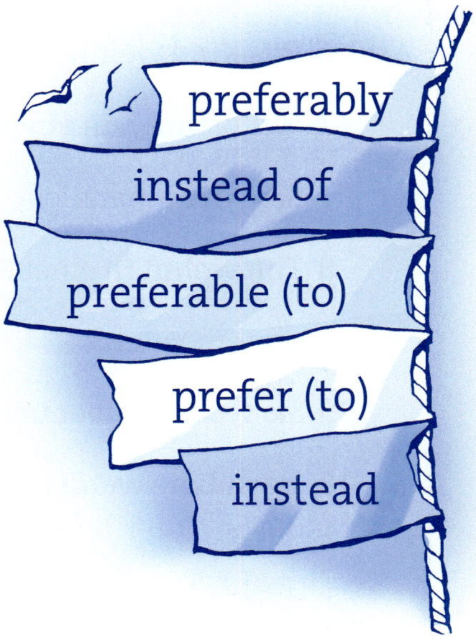

9 What is it?

Schreibe die englische und die deutsche Bezeichnung neben die Satzzeichen.

1 ! ____________ ____________

2 - ____________ ____________

3 : ____________ ____________

4 ? ____________ ____________

5) ____________ ____________

6 . ____________ ____________

New words ▸ *p. 19 | VOCABULARY p. 214*

1 Unsere Nachbarn **kümmern** sich **um** unsere Katze, wenn wir im Urlaub sind.	Our neighbours ______ our cat when we're on holiday.
2 Du kannst mein Fahrrad haben. Ich **brauche** es **nicht mehr**.	You can have my bike. I ______ it ______.
3 Werdet ihr jemals aus Italien **zurückkehren**?	Will you ever ______ from Italy?
4 Ich gehe nicht gern am Samstag einkaufen, weil die Geschäfte da so **überfüllt** sind.	I don't like shopping on Saturday because the shops are so ______ then.
5 Ich habe ein paar schöne Schuhe im **Schaufenster** gesehen.	I saw a nice pair of shoes in the ______.
6 Das Kind weinte und sah **verängstigt** aus.	The child cried and looked ______.
7 Wir wohnen in **einer Wohnung mit zwei Schlafzimmern**.	We live in ______.
8 Tim wohnt in einer **Sozialwohnung** mit seinem Vater.	Tim lives in a ______ with his father.
9 Sie wohnen **über** uns.	They live ______ us.
10 **Irgendwie** werden wir schon klarkommen.	We'll manage ______.

10 What are the right words?

Setze die richtigen Wörter in die Sätze ein. Achte auf die richtige Form.

1 I don't want to walk home on my own.
It ______ me.

2 Are you ______ dogs?

3 Lots of companies have closed down here recently.
It's ______.

4 The little boy looked ______,
but he didn't want to tell us what was
______ him.

5 Unemployment has reached a ______
level in lots of African countries.

New words ▸ *pp. 20–21 | VOCABULARY pp. 214–215*

1 Darf ich mir die Suppe in der **Mikrowelle erhitzen**?	May I ______________ the soup in the ______________?
2 Bitte **mach es dir gemütlich**.	Please ______________ ______________.
3 Er wusste nicht, zu welchem **Volk** er gehörte.	He didn't know which ______________ he belonged to.
4 Ich **habe eine Entscheidung gefällt**: Ich möchte Koch werden.	I ______________: I want to become a cook.
5 Es war ganz **still** um mich herum.	It was completely ______________ around me.
6 Ich **war im Begriff** zu gehen, als Tom an meinen Tisch kam.	I ______________ to go when Tom came to my table.
7 **Von nun an** musst du dein Zimmer selbst aufräumen.	______________ you have to tidy your room yourself.
8 Du brauchst einen **Pass**, wenn du nach Afrika fliegen willst.	You need a ______________ if you want to fly to Africa.
9 Ich verabschiedete mich und **umarmte** meinen Freund.	I said goodbye and ______________ my friend.
10 Eine **Charakterisierung** der Hauptperson	A ______________ of the main character
11 **Charakterisiere** die Frauen des Theaterstücks.	______________ the women in the play.
12 Ich erwartete eine positive **Antwort** auf meine Bewerbung, aber sie blieb aus.	I expected a positive ______________ to my application, but it never came.

11 Opposites

Finde das Gegenteil.

1 high ◂▸ ______________

2 below ◂▸ ______________

3 employment ◂▸ ______________

4 minority ◂▸ ______________

New words ▸ *p. 19 | VOCABULARY pp. 215–216*

! *Wenn du den Text auf den Seiten 19–21 in deinem Schülerbuch gelesen und die zusätzlichen Wörter daraus gelernt hast, kannst du diese* ***New words*** *bearbeiten.*

1°	England und Frankreich sind durch einen **Tunnel** verbunden.	England and France are connected by a ____________________.
2°	Der Fußboden **war** mit Spielsachen **bedeckt**.	The floor ____________________ in toys.
3°	Sein **plötzlicher** Tod schockierte uns.	His ____________________ death shocked us.
4°	Ich konnte nur einen **kurzen Blick** auf meine Geschenke werfen.	I only caught a ____________________ of my presents.
5°	Ihre Beschimpfungen **hallten** in meinem Kopf **wider**.	Their taunts ____________________ in my head.
6°	Ich muss mich **beeilen**, da mein Zug bald fährt.	I have to ____________________ because my train is leaving soon.
7°	**Ab und zu** essen wir Pizza in einem italienischen Restaurant.	We eat pizza in an Italian restaurant ____________________.
8°	Er wollte dich **gewiss** nicht verletzen.	He ____________________ didn't want to hurt you.
9°	Tom hat dein Auto nicht genommen **und ich auch nicht**.	Tom didn't take your car ____________________ ____________________.
10°	Sie **schlang** ihr Mittagessen **herunter** und ging zurück an ihren Schreibtisch.	She ____________________ her lunch and went back to her desk.
11°	Bitte komm nach der Schule **direkt** nach Hause.	Please come ____________________ home from school.
12°	Sie kauften zwei **Packungen** Milch.	They bought two ____________________ of milk.

New words ▸ *pp. 20–21 | VOCABULARY pp. 216–217*

1° Gibt es noch **übriggebliebenen** Kuchen?	Is there any ____________ cake?
2° Die Blätter **waren gelb geworden**.	The leaves ____________.
3° Ich mag nur grüne **Oliven**.	I only like green ____________.
4° **Ananas** wachsen in tropischen Gebieten.	____________ grow in tropical areas.
5° Als ich die Fotos sah, **wanderten** meine Gedanken zu unserem letzten Urlaub.	When I saw the photos my thoughts ____________ to our last holiday.
6° Anne **seufzte**, als sie die Unordnung sah.	Anne ____________ when she saw the mess.
7° Ich wünsche mir einen goldenen **Ring**.	I'd like to have a gold ____________.
8° Du siehst müde und **blass** aus.	You're looking tired and ____________.
9° Das Eis hier ist zu teuer und **außerdem** hattest du heute schon eines.	The ice cream is too expensive here, and ____________, you already had one today.
10° Wasch bitte deine **schmutzige** Hose.	Please wash your ____________ trousers.
11° Ich wasche gern **Geschirr** ab.	I like doing the ____________.
12° Bitte leere den **Mülleimer** raus.	Please empty the ____________.
13° Ich **mühe** mich gerade mit der Bedienung meines neuen Telefons **ab**.	I'm ____________ with my new phone.
14° Viele Leute haben **Angst** vor dem Fliegen.	A lot of people have a ____________ of flying.
15° Sie **wendete sich ab** und fing an zu weinen.	She ____________ and started to cry.
16° Tränen **strömten** über ihr Gesicht.	Tears ____________ down her face.
17° Sie **zitterte** am ganzen Körper.	Her whole body ____________.
18° Habt ihr **finanzielle Schwierigkeiten**?	Are you in ____________ ____________?
19° Ich möchte etwas **mit dir besprechen**.	I want to ____________ something ____________.
20° Als die Schlange mich biss, bekam ich **panische Angst**.	When the snake bit me I was full of ____________.
21° **Wo** liegt denn das Dorf **überhaupt**?	____________ is the village ____________?

New words ▸ p. 21 | *VOCABULARY p. 217*

1° Wir haben uns billige Flugtickets gekauft **und ab ging's nach** Kreta.	We bought cheap flight tickets ________________ ________________ Crete.
2° Die Serie soll gut sein, aber ich habe bisher nur **Teile** davon gesehen.	The series is supposed to be good, but I've only seen ________________ so far.
3° **Fernsehen** interessiert mich nicht.	I'm not interested in ________________.
4° **Haben sie überhaupt Straßen?**	________________
5° Wir werden **für immer** in London bleiben.	We'll stay in London ________________.

! *Wenn du den Text auf den Seiten 19–21 in deinem Schülerbuch gelesen und die zusätzlichen Wörter daraus gelernt hast, kannst du die **Aufgabe 12** bearbeiten.*

12 Word labyrinth

Übersetze die Wörter ins Englische und trage sie in das Wortlabyrinth ein. Die Anfangsbuchstaben helfen dir dabei. Das Lösungswort findest du in den grauen Feldern.

seufzen – blass – schmutzig – Mülleimer – Angst – sich beeilen – sicherlich – bedecken – außerdem – Schwierigkeit – kämpfen

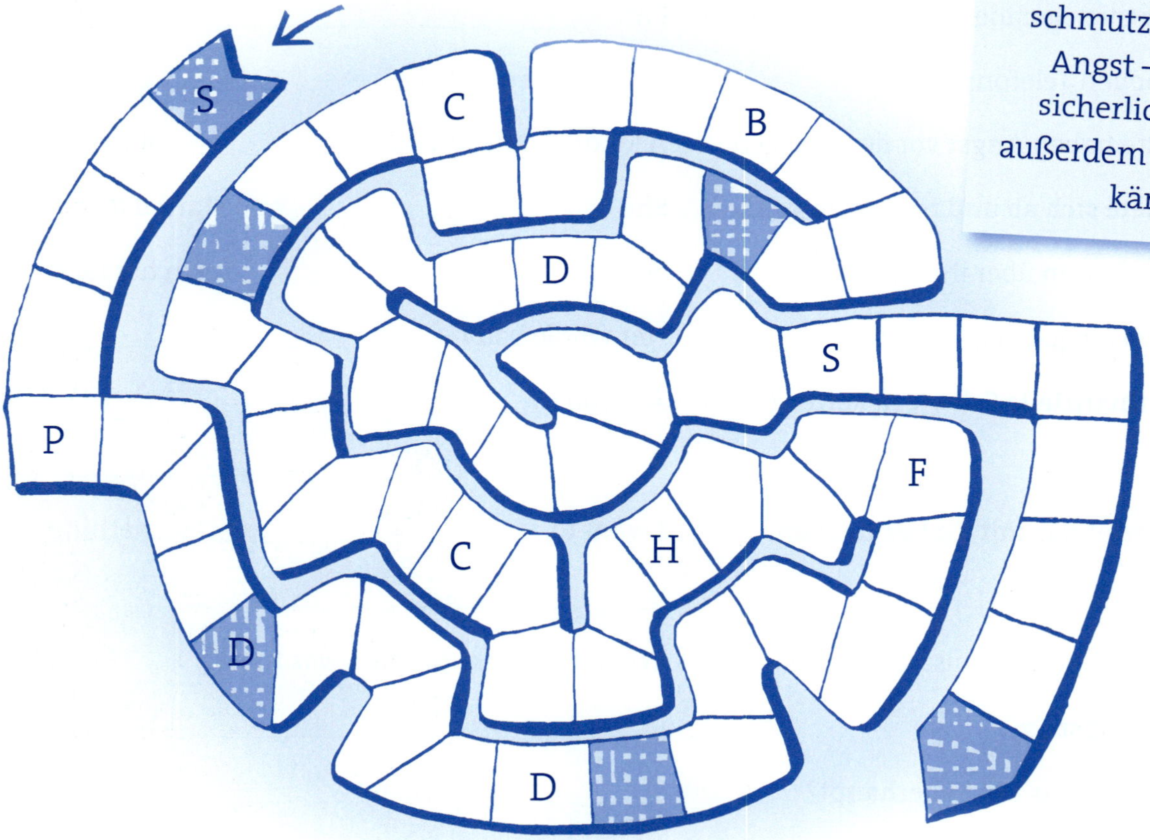

Lösungswort: ________________

New words ▸ *p. 22 | VOCABULARY pp. 217–218*

1 Die **Giraffe** ist das höchste Tier der Welt. In Afrika kann man **Giraffen** in freier Wildbahn sehen.	The ______________ is the tallest animal in the world. In Africa you can see ______________ in the wild.
2 Bitte **fülle** das Formular **aus**.	Please ______________ the form.
3 Schreibe die fehlenden Wörter in die **Lücken**.	Write the missing words in the ______________.
4 Hat unser Hotel freies **WLAN**?	Is there free ______________ in our hotel?
5 **Einchecken** ist zwischen 10 und 20 Uhr möglich.	______________ is possible between 10 am and 8 pm.
6 Die **Anlagen** sind einfach aber sauber.	The ______________ are basic but clean.
7 Ein **Dieb** hat mir die Tasche gestohlen. Schilder hatten uns vor **Dieben** gewarnt.	A ______________ stole my bag. Signs had warned us about ______________.
8 Sie **arbeiten** Tag und Nacht.	They are ______________ day and night.
9 Auf dem Flughafen darfst du deine Tasche nie **unbeaufsichtigt** lassen.	You mustn't leave your bag ______________ at the airport.
10 Bitte **entfernen** Sie ihr Fahrzeug. Es blockiert die Einfahrt.	Please ______________ your vehicle. It's blocking the entrance.
11 Komm **sofort** nach Hause!	Come home ______________!
12 Es **wird** möglicherweise vernichtet.	It ______________ be destroyed.

13 Scrambled words

Setze die richtigen Wörter aus dem Reservoir in die Sätze ein.

1 The police caught two ______________ at the station.

2 Never leave your bags ______________ at the airport.

3 I called Rex and he came ______________.

4 The ______________ at our hotel were fantastic.

New words ▸ *p. 23 | VOCABULARY p. 218*

1 Wie viel Geld hast du in deiner **Brieftasche**?	How much money do you have in your ______________?
2 Sandra **fehlt** heute.	Sandra is ______________ing today.
3 Jeder Deutsche über 18 muss einen **Ausweis** bei sich haben.	Any German over 18 must carry ______________ on him or her.
4 Mit einem **Schülerausweis** kommst du Rabatt.	You'll get reductions with your ______________ ______________
5 Wir müssen das unserem Lehrer **melden**.	We have to ______________ this to our teacher.

14 Crossword puzzle

Trage die Wörter in das Kreuzworträtsel ein.

1 the state of being poor
2 another word for the verb "work"
3 the part along the side or end of something
5 another word for "quiet"
6 measure how heavy something is
7 another word for "really" or "honestly"
9 another word for "reaction" or "answer"
11 → 100 years
11 ↓ anything that lives and is not a plant
12 a space between two things
13 not able to think clearly
14 take sth. or sb. away or off
15 move your foot up and forward
16 chose sb. for a certain position
17 ◂▸ high
18 working well

⑧

④

⑩

New words ▸ *pp. 24–25 | VOCABULARY p. 218*

1 **Vermittlung, Sprachmittlung**	______________________
2 **Historische** Ereignisse interessieren mich sehr.	I'm very interested in ______________ events.
3 Wofür steht dieses **Denkmal**?	What's this ______________ for?
4 Wir **stellen** Handtücher zur **Verfügung**.	We ______________ towels.
5 Es gibt einen **täglichen** Busverkehr.	There is a ______________ bus service.
6 Wie hoch ist der **Mindestlohn** in Großbritannien?	What's the ______________ wage in Great Britain?
7 Kannst du mir helfen, das Schild zu **übersetzen**?	Can you help me to ______________ this sign?
8 **Eines Tages** werde ich berühmt sein.	______________ I'll be famous.
9 Ich habe deine **Reaktion** nicht ganz verstanden.	I didn't quite understand your ______________.
10 Diese Bilder werden in deinen **Gedanken haften bleiben**.	These picture will ______________ in your ______________.
11 Kennst du eine wirkungsvolle **Methode**, Vokabeln zu lernen?	Do you know an effective ______________ to learn vocabulary?
12 Er spricht den **Filmkommentar**.	He does the ______________.
13 Die Dokumentation enthielt beeindruckende **Nahaufnahmen**.	The documentary contained some amazing ______________.
14 Kleine Menschengruppen und Einzelpersonen werden gern in der **Halbtotale** gezeigt.	Small groups of people and single persons are often filmed in a ______________.
15 Wir müssen noch eine **Aufnahme** machen.	We have to take another ______________.
16 Wir sehen den Hauptdarsteller in der **Totale**.	We can see the main character in a ______________.
17 Lass uns die Plätze **tauschen**.	Let's ______________ places.

15 Bits and pieces

Verbinde die Silben, um englische Wörter zu bilden. Übersetze die Wörter ins Deutsche.

1	medium	day	______	______
2	close-	card	______	______
3	prime	place	______	______
4	long	up	______	______
5	take	shot	______	______
6	voice-	minister	______	______
7	some	about	______	______
8	news	over	______	______
9	student	item	______	______
10	care	shot	______	______

16 First letter – last letter

Der letzte Buchstabe jedes Wortes ist gleichzeitig der erste Buchstabe des nächsten Wortes.

1 (sich) umarmen
2 wählen
3 typisch
4 niedrig, tief
5 wiegen
6 (sich) umarmen
7 Giraffen
8 tauschen
9 (an)bieten, zur Verfügung stellen
10 effektiv, wirksam
11 Rand, Kante
12 Echo
13 Gelegenheit, Möglichkeit, Chance

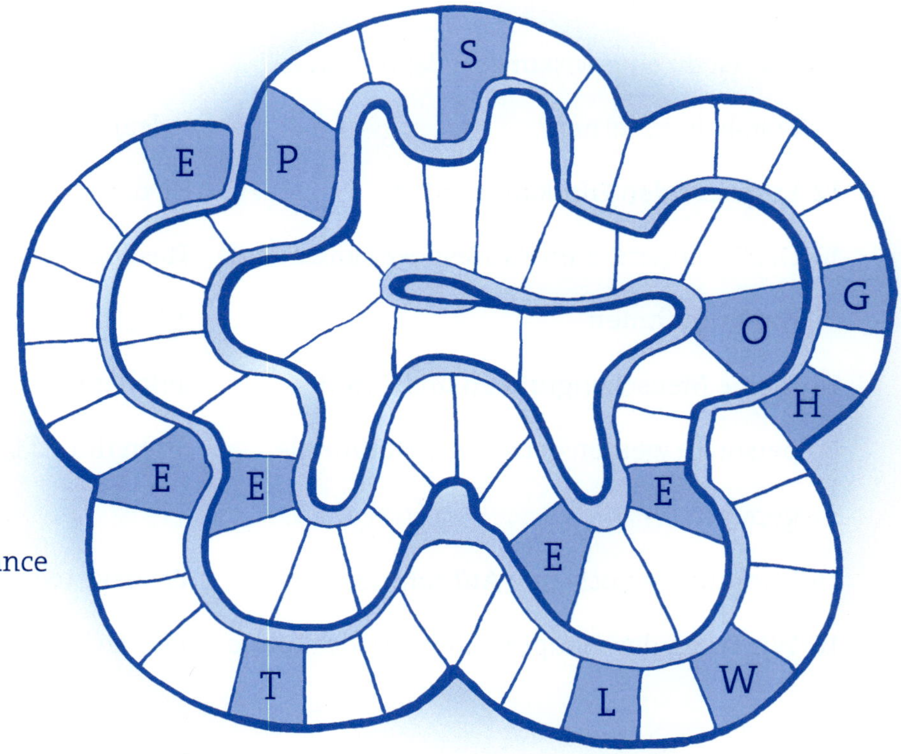

New words MORE CHALLENGE ▸ *p. 30 | VOCABULARY pp. 236–237*

1° **Wildern** ist illegal.	____________________ing is illegal.
2° Die Jugendarbeitslosigkeit in Spanien hat **ein Rekordniveau** erreicht.	Youth unemployment in Spain is ____________________.
3° Das hat zur **Folge**, dass viele junge Spanier woanders Arbeit suchen.	As a ____________, lots of young Spanish people look for work elsewhere.
4° **Bestimmte** Jobs sind besonders schwer zu bekommen.	________________ jobs are especially difficult to get.
5° Orang-Utans sind vom **Aussterben** bedroht.	Orang-utans are at risk of ____________.
6° Er muss einen **Anti**-Aggressionskurs besuchen.	He has to attend an ________________ aggression course.
7° Der **Mond** scheint sehr hell heute Abend.	The ____________ is very bright tonight.
8° Mein Großvater ist auf der **Jagd**.	My grandad is on the ____________.
9° Ein hoher Zaun **umgab** den Garten.	A high fence ____________ the garden.
10° Ich kann meine Familie bis ins 18. Jahrhundert **zurückverfolgen**.	I can ________________ my family back to the 18th century.
11° **Bewaffnete** Soldaten kontrollierten die Grenze.	________________ soldiers controlled the frontier.
12° Wir **konfrontierten** ihn mit unseren Ideen.	We ____________ him with our ideas.
13° Wie unser Lehrer es **ausdrückt**: „Besser spät als nie."	As our teacher ________________ it: "Better late than never."
14° Ich muss arbeiten. **Deshalb** musst du allein ins Kino gehen.	I have to work. ____________ you have to go to the cinema on your own.
15° Ich arbeite immer zwei Wochen **am Stück**. Danach habe ich zwei Wochen frei.	I work two weeks ________________. Then I'm free for two weeks.
16° Sie ging **trotz** ihrer Erkältung zur Arbeit.	She went to work ____________ her cold.

17 Word search

Kreise 30 Wörter, die du in Unit 1 gelernt hast, in dem Gitter ein. Die Fotos und die Bilderrahmen helfen dir. Du musst in 8 Richtungen suchen (→ ← ↓ ↑ ↖ ↗ ↘ ↙).

A	B	C	D	D	E	F	G	H	W	N	R	U	T	E	R
I	J	T	R	A	N	S	L	A	T	E	K	L	M	N	O
P	Q	R	M	I	N	D	L	S	R	A	I	N	B	O	W
M	T	U	V	L	W	L	T	E	C	H	N	I	Q	U	E
I	E	T	X	Y	E	Z	A	P	R	O	V	I	D	E	P
N	C	D	N	T	E	S	I	L	E	N	T	F	P	W	A
I	C	H	I	E	D	B	A	K	E	R	D	L	M	I	S
M	U	I	F	A	M	G	H	K	I	I	A	W	E	L	S
U	R	S	P	C	T	U	C	J	A	T	K	E	M	D	P
M	R	T	E	C	L	I	N	M	F	M	N	I	O	L	O
O	E	O	O	E	T	P	O	O	Q	R	S	G	R	I	R
T	N	R	P	S	U	N	R	N	M	V	W	H	Y	F	T
X	C	I	L	S	D	M	I	C	R	O	W	A	V	E	Y
Z	Y	C	E	H	C	I	R	T	S	O	E	D	G	E	A
C	H	A	R	A	C	T	E	R	I	Z	A	T	I	O	N
C	I	L	B	U	P	A	S	U	B	U	R	B	X	B	C

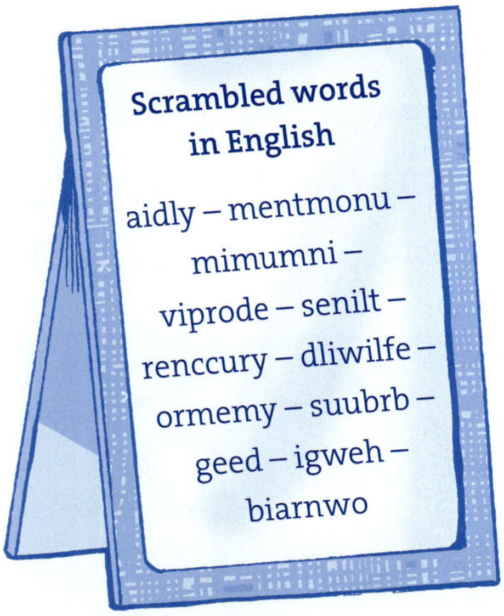

Take a stand!

Unit 2

New words
▸ pp. 32–33 | VOCABULARY p. 219

1 Es ist wichtig, **gegen** Gewalt an Kindern **Stellung** zu **beziehen**.	It's important to ______________________ ______________ violence towards children.
2 Mona **kreiert** wunderbare Nachtische.	Mona ________________ fantastic desserts.

New words
▸ p. 34 | VOCABULARY p. 219

1 politischer **Aktivismus**	political ______________________________
2 Tausende Menschen nahmen an einer **Demonstration** gegen Studiengebühren teil.	Thousands of people took part in a _________________ against university fees.
3 Der **Protest** dauert schon einige Monate.	The ____________________ has been going on for some months.
4 **Heutzutage** ist es leicht, auch über größere Entfernungen in Kontakt zu bleiben.	______________________ it's easy to stay in touch in spite of huge distances.
5 Bitte **retuschieren** Sie meine Fotos nicht. Ich möchte so aussehen wie immer.	Please don't _________________ my photos. I want to look the same as I normally do.
6 Ich habe gerade eine **Petition** zum Schutz der Delfine unterschrieben.	I've just signed a ___________________ for the protection of dolphins.
7 Wir brauchen 1.000 **Unterschriften**.	We need 1,000 _________________________.
8 Wer hat hier die **Macht**?	Who is in _______________________ here?
9 Wie viele Leute waren auf der Demonstration? – Die Polizei **schätzt** ungefähr 20.000.	How many people attended the demonstration? – The police _____________ about 20,000.
10 Sitz nicht tatenlos herum, sondern **beteilige dich an** sozialen Projekten.	Don't sit around doing nothing: ___________ _______________________ social projects.
11 Ohne das Internet könnten sich **Meme** nicht so schnell verbreiten.	______________________ couldn't spread as fast without the internet.

New words ▸ *p. 34 | VOCABULARY p. 219*

1 Der Koch **wies darauf hin**, dass er nur Bioprodukte verwendet.	The cook ______________ that he only used organic products.
2 Wir fuhren **über** Halle nach Leipzig.	We drove to Leipzig ______________ Halle.
3 Internet**trolle** hinterlassen oft sehr **verletzende** Kommentare.	Internet ______________ often leave very ______________ comments.
4 Ich habe **eine Menge** Schuhe, die ich nicht mehr trage.	I have ______________ shoes that I don't wear anymore.

New words ▸ *p. 35 | VOCABULARY p. 219*

1 Bitte antworte in **vollständigen** Sätzen.	Please answer in ______________ sentences.
2 Mein Bruder hat mir geholfen, **das Problem** zu **lösen**.	My brother helped me to ______________ ______________.

1 Find the words

Trage die Wörter in das Kammrätsel ein. Wie lautet das Lösungswort in den blauen Feldern?

1 Another expression for "lots of"
2 An idea, image, video etc. which people get to know via the internet
3 Say how long, high, big etc. you think sth. is
4 Say or show that you are against sth.
5 Your name in the way you write it
6 Find the answer to a problem
7 A letter or a web document that people sign to ask for sth.
8 Another word for "painful"
9 Going through a place on your way from A to B = going ... that place
10 Make something new
11 To do sth. to a photo to make it look better
12 Another word for "energy" or "strength"
13 To tell or show sth.

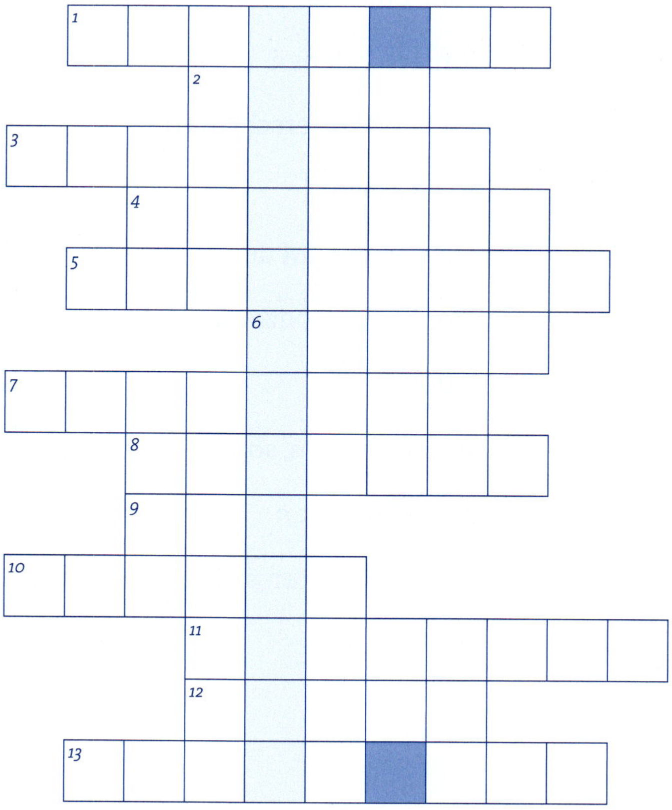

New words ▸ *pp. 36–37 | VOCABULARY p. 220*

1 Ich **nehme** meine Schulaufgaben **wichtig**.	I ____________ my school work.
2 Konrad Adenauer war der erste **Bundeskanzler** der Bundesrepublik Deutschland.	Konrad Adenauer was the first ____________ of the Federal Republic of Germany.
3 Margaret Thatcher war die erste **Premierministerin** des vereinigten Königreichs.	Margaret Thatcher was the first female ________ ____________ of the United Kingdom.
4 Ich interessiere mich sehr für **Politik**.	I'm very interested in ____________.
5 Bitte **achten** Sie **auf** die Durchsagen.	Please ____________ the announcements.
6 Seine **Rente** war nicht sehr hoch, da er nie viel verdient hat.	His ____________ wasn't very high as he never earned a lot of money.
7 Ich kann mich nicht an ihren Namen erinnern. Es ist **eine Ewigkeit** her, seit ich sie das letzte Mal gesehen habe.	I can't remember her name. It's ____________ since I last saw her.
8 Manchmal ist es schwer zu verstehen, **worum es in der Politik geht**.	Sometimes it's hard to understand ____________ ____________.
9 Ich bin sicher, dass er mir mein Handy gestohlen hat, aber ich kann es nicht **beweisen**.	I'm sure he stole my mobile, but I can't ____________ it.
10 Man hat die **Wahl** zwischen Nudeln, Reis und Kartoffeln.	There is a ____________ between pasta, rice and potatoes.
11 **Hast** du **ein Mitspracherecht**, auf welche Schule du gehen möchtest?	Do you ____________ the school you want to go to?
12 Freie Wahlen sind ein wichtiges Instrument der **Demokratie**.	Free elections are an important instrument of ____________.
13 Sie studiert Jura und will **Politikerin** werden.	She's studying law and wants to become a ____________.

2 Word building

Finde das fehlende Wort und übersetze alles ins Deutsche.

Verb	German	Nomen	German
		activism	
protest			
		signature	
		completion	
choose			

New words ▸ *p. 38 | VOCABULARY p. 221*

1 Die Polizei fing den **Räuber**. — The police caught the ______.

2 Die Arbeiter **forderten** eine gerechte Bezahlung. — The workers ______ fair pay.

3 Die Belegschaft **pries** ihre Chefin **für** ihren Humor und ihre Menschlichkeit. — The staff ______ their boss for her good humour and her humanity.

4 Ich **bin** beim Aufräumen **auf** ein paar alte Fotos **gestoßen**. — I ______ some old photos when I tidied my flat.

5 Meine Eltern kamen als **Flüchtlinge** nach Deutschland. — My parents came to Germany as ______.

6 Ihr Kampf ums **Überleben** ist **bemerkenswert**. — Their fight for ______ is ______.

7 Sie hat viele Jahre auf der **Bühne** gestanden. — She's been on the ______ for many years.

8 Der Bankraub war gestern die wichtigste **Pressemeldung**. — The bank robbery was the most important ______ yesterday.

9 Das Stück wurde für vier **Darsteller** geschrieben. — The play was written for four ______.

10 Bitte hör zu und **unterbrich** mich nicht. — Please listen and don't ______ me.

3 Linking

Verbinde die richtigen deutschen und englischen Sätze miteinander.

1 I really care about my cat.
2 Who cares about your cat?
3 Do you care?
4 I didn't care about cats before I got mine.
5 You should care about your animals.
6 My neighbours don't like cats. – Who cares?

A Katzen waren mir egal, bevor ich meine bekam.
B Du solltest dich um deine Tiere kümmern.
C Wen interessiert deine Katze?
D Meine Nachbarn mögen keine Katzen. – Na und?
E Meine Katze liegt mir sehr am Herzen.
F Interessiert dich das?

4 Lost words

Setze die richtigen Wörter in die Sätze ein.

1 Our teachers always point ________________ that it's important to get involved ________________ social projects.
2 There are loads ________________ opportunities in our community.
3 First you should find out what you really care ________________.
4 Please pay attention ________________ what I'm saying.
5 Will you let your parents have a say ________________ your decision?
6 Last week I came ________________ a really interesting project.
7 How did your parents react ________________ it?

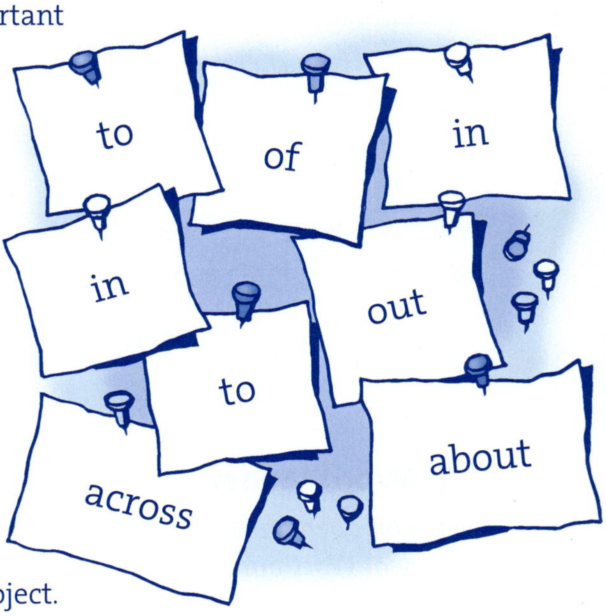

5 Definitions

Welche Wörter werden hier gesucht?

1 The money people get after they have retired from work: ________________
2 To say or show successfully that something is true: ________________
3 A system of government where the people elect their leaders: ________________
4 A person who works in the government: ________________
5 Someone who steals from a person or place using violence: ________________
6 A person who must leave his or her country because of danger: ________________

New words ▸ *pp. 39–40 | VOCABULARY pp. 221–222*

1 Das Konzert **war** noch **im Gange**, als ich nach Hause gehen musste.	The concert ________ still ________ when I had to go home.
2 Wann wird das nächste Konzert **stattfinden**?	When will the next concert ________?
3 Wir **sammeln Geld** für unser Schulfest.	We're ________ing ________ for our school party.
4 Ich habe in diesem Sommer drei **wunderbare** Wochen in Cornwall verbracht.	I spent three ________ weeks in Cornwall this summer.
5 Hänsel und Gretel fanden ein **Pfefferkuchen**haus im Wald.	Hansel and Gretel found a ________ house in the woods.
6 Dein Kuchen ist **köstlich**, aber ich kann nicht noch ein Stück davon essen.	Your cake is ________, but I can't eat another piece.
7 London ist im **Vergleich** zu Berlin sehr teuer.	London is very expensive in ________ with Berlin.
8 Wir waren Pizza essen und **hinterher** sind wir spazieren gegangen.	We ate pizza and ________ we went for a walk.

6 Word ladder

Gehe von oben nach unten und verändere bei jedem Wort nur einen Buchstaben.

1 I like Sam, but I don't want to ___ him.

2 Sorry I'm ___. I missed the bus.

3 I like meat, but I ___ fish.

4 Your flight is now boarding at ___ 7.

5 Let's play a ___.

6 She ___ from Sydney 20 years ago.

7 I really ___ about my little brother.

8 Philip sent me a birthday ___.

New words ▸ *pp. 41–43 | VOCABULARY pp. 222–223*

1 Ich werde dich **ewig** lieben.	I'll love you ____________.
2 Ich lese gerade einen **Roman** über Trolle.	I'm reading a ____________ about trolls.
3 **Nadel** und Faden	____________ and thread
4 Zwei Männer **kamen** auf sie **zu**.	Two men were ____________ing their ______.
5 **Scheinwerferlicht** erhellte den Weg.	____________ lit the path.
6 Ich suche eine **Mitfahrgelegenheit** nach Rom.	I'm looking for a ____________ to Rome.
7 Du musst **verrückt** sein, ohne Geld nach London zu fliegen.	You must be ____________ flying to London without any money.
8 Der Räuber wurde nach einer kurzen **Verfolgungsjagd** gefasst.	The robber was caught after a short ____________.
9 "Lass das die **Bullen** nicht sehen!"	"Don't let the ____________ see this!"
10 **Schalte** bitte das Radio **ein**.	____________ the radio ________, please.
11 Wir hörten die **Sirenen**.	We heard the ____________.
12 **Leuchte** mal mit der Taschenlampe.	____________ your torch.
13 Ich wurde bei einem Auto**unfall** verletzt.	I was hurt in a car ____________.
14 Ein LKW **ist mit** unserem Auto **zusammengestoßen**.	A lorry ____________ our car.
15 Dem Feuer folgte eine **Explosion**.	The fire was followed by an ____________.
16 Viele Arbeiter hatten schlimme **Brandverletzungen**.	Lots of workers had bad ____________.
17 Als Tom um Mitternacht nicht zu Hause war, waren seine Eltern **beunruhigt**.	When Tom wasn't at home at midnight, his parents were ____________.
18 **Im Laufe der Zeit** verbesserte sich sein Englisch.	His English improved ____________.
19 **Joyriding** ist sehr gefährlich.	____________ is very dangerous.
20 Ich wollte nach Paris fliegen, **habe es mir** aber dann **anders überlegt**.	I wanted to fly to Paris, but then ____________ ____________.

7 Word web

Finde die Wörter, die in das Spinnennetz passen. Alle haben sechs Buchstaben und enden auf -e.

1 Not like anybody or anything else:
2 All the persons who belong to a particular country:
3 Take someone or something away from a place:
4 Make something new:
5 The opportunity to choose from different things:
6 Say that someone or something is very good:

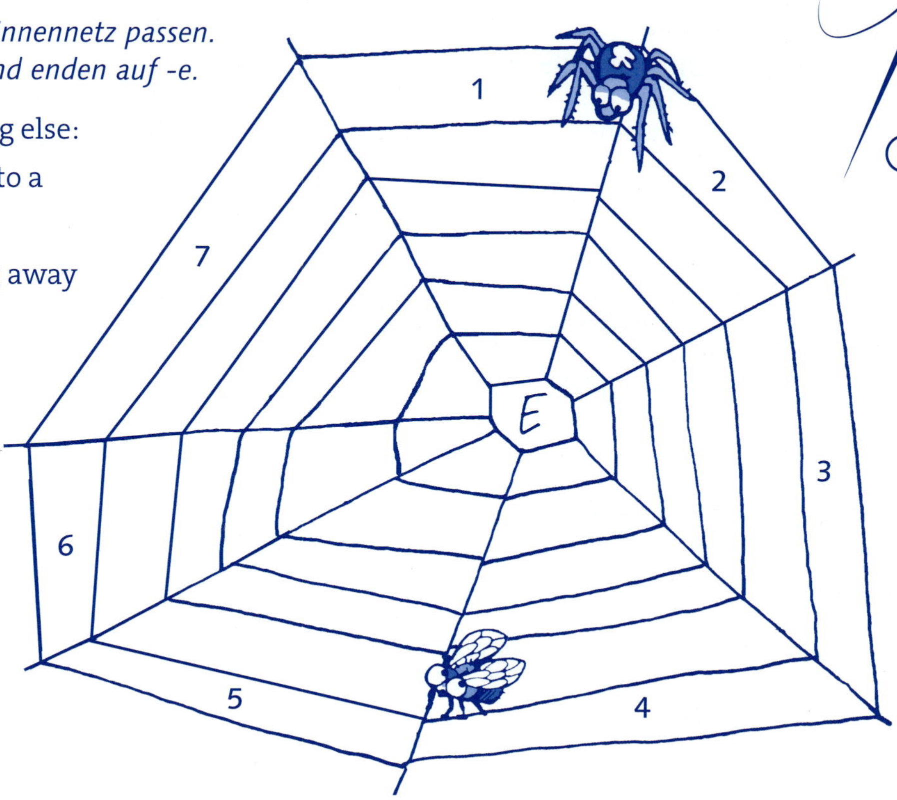

8 Word pairs

Welche Wörter passen zusammen?

be – change – crash – get – pay – point – put on – raise – solve

_______ involved in

_______ sth. out

_______ a problem

_______ attention

_______ the radio

_______ into a car

_______ one's mind

_______ in progress

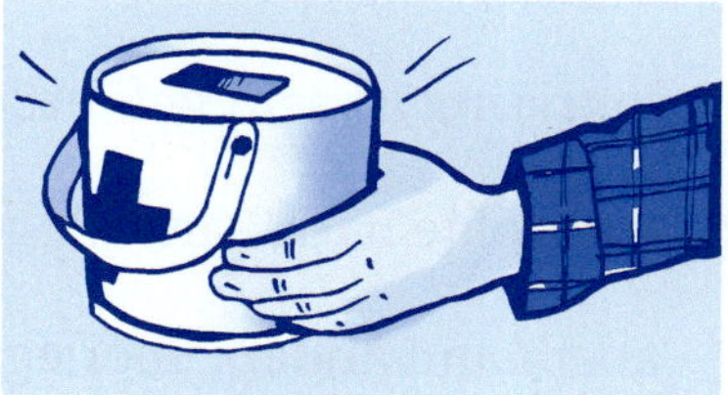

_______ money

9 Word labyrinth

Übersetze die Wörter ins Englische. Trage die englischen Wörter in das Labyrinth ein. Die Anfangsbuchstaben helfen dir. Das Lösungswort findest du in den blauen Feldern.

lecker – bemerkenswert – wunderbar – verletzend – vollständig – unbeaufsichtigt – politisch – still

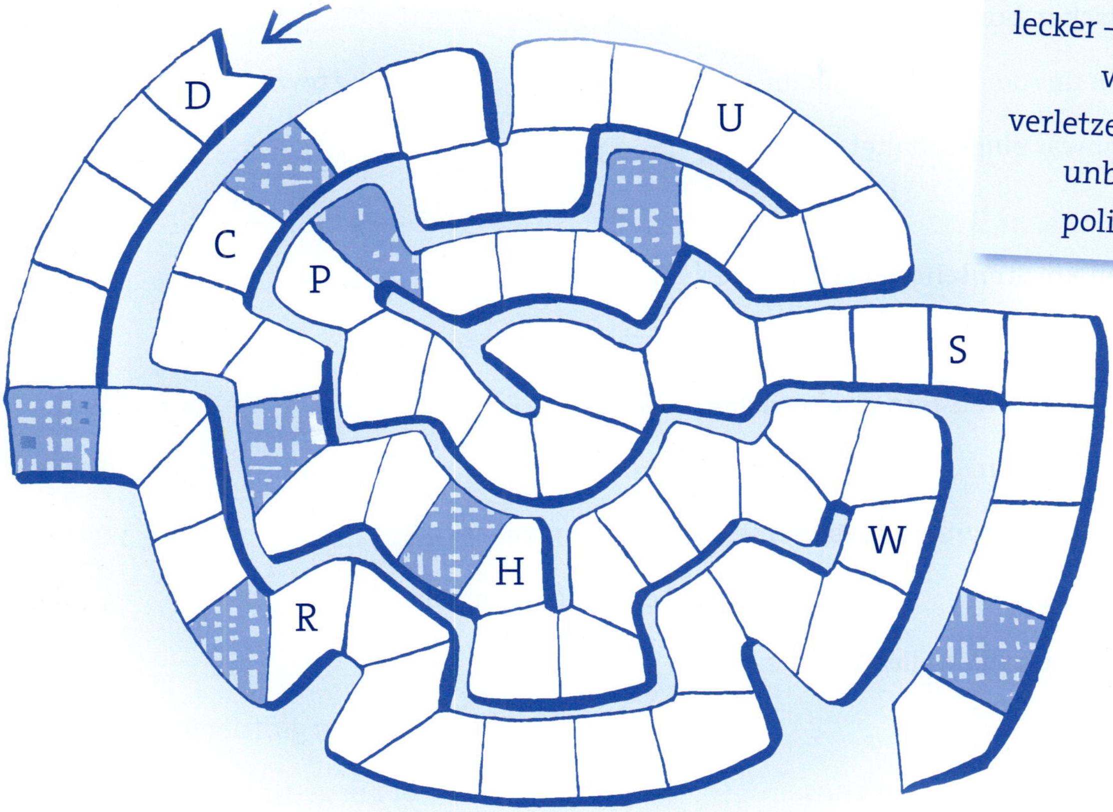

Lösungswort: ____________________

New words ▸ *p. 41 | VOCABULARY pp. 223–224*

! *Wenn du den Text auf den Seiten 41–43 in deinem Schülerbuch gelesen und die zusätzlichen Wörter daraus gelernt hast, kannst du die* ***New words*** *auf dieser und den beiden folgenden Seiten und* ***Aufgabe 10*** *und* ***11*** *bearbeiten.*

1° Nach dem Konzert **gingen** wir alle **Richtung** Bahnhof.	After the concert we all ____________________ for the station.
2° Kannst du mich **zum Bahnhof begleiten**?	Can you ____________ me ________ the station?
3° Wir können eine **Abkürzung durch** den Park nehmen.	We can ____________________ the park.
4° Tom und ich kommen aus derselben **Wohnsiedlung**.	Tom and I come from the same ____________________.
5° Das **Hochhaus** wird 25 Stockwerke hoch sein.	The ____________________ will be 25 storeys high.

New words ▸ *pp. 41–42 | VOCABULARY p. 224*

1° Sie bemerkte das Auto erst, als sie die Reifen **quietschen** hörte.	She only noticed the car when she heard the tyres ________________.
2° Wir **näherten** uns der Stadt von Süden.	We __________ the town from the south.
3° **Das Fernlicht war eingeschaltet.**	____________________ ____________________
4° Ein Auto **hielt am Straßenrand an** und drei Frauen stiegen aus.	A car ________________ and three women got out.
5° Wir versuchten unsere Eltern zu **überreden**, einen Hund zu kaufen.	We tried to ____________ our parents to buy a dog.
6° Meine Schwester war **wütend**, als ich ihr Handy fallen ließ.	My sister was ____________ when I dropped her mobile.
7° **Ich soll** dir nicht erzählen, **dass** Tom eine neue Freundin hat.	__________ not __________ tell you that Tom has a new girlfriend.
8° Hör auf zu **rasen**, oder ich steige aus.	Stop ________ or I'm getting out of the car.
9° In unserer Straße gibt es jetzt eine **Bremsschwelle**, um sie sicherer zu machen.	There's a ________________ in our street to make it safer.
10° Ich mache mit meinen **Kumpeln** Urlaub.	I'm going on holiday with my __________.
11° Der Schnitt hat eine große **Narbe** in meinem Gesicht hinterlassen.	The cut left a big __________ on my face.
12° Als er das Polizeifahrzeug hinter sich sah, **gab** er **Gas**.	When he saw the police car behind him, he ____________________.
13° Wo bist du? – **Direkt hinter** dir!	Where are you? – ____________ you!
14° Bieg an der **Kreuzung** rechts ab.	Turn right at the ______________.
15° Du kannst **gleich** reingehen.	You can go ________________ in.
16° Der Fahrer **beschädigte** zwei andere Autos.	The driver ____________ two other cars.
17° Nach dem Unfall war er eine Weile **bewusstlos**.	After the accident he was ____________ for a while.

New words ▸ *pp. 42–43 | VOCABULARY pp. 224–225*

1° Wir zogen ihm das **blutige** Hemd aus.	We took off his ______________ shirt.
2° Der Räuber **griff nach** meinem Handy und rannte damit weg.	The robber ______________ my mobile and ran away with it.
3° Zwei **Rettungssanitäter** schoben mich auf einer **Trage** zum Krankenwagen.	Two ______________ pushed me to the ambulance on a ______________.
4° Maria brachte mich auf **schnellstem Weg zum** Flughafen.	Maria ______________ me ______ the airport.
5° Sam bereitet mir oft **schlaflose** Nächte.	Sam often causes me ______________ nights.
6° Hast du Hunger, **Liebling**?	Are you hungry, ______________?
7° Mit einem gebrochenen Bein **musst** du **dich schonen**.	______________ with a broken leg.
8° **Lehn dich zurück** und genieße die Musik.	______________ and enjoy the music.
9° Ich möchte **Krankenschwester** werden und in einem großen Krankenhaus arbeiten.	I want to become a ______________ and work in a big hospital.
10° Wir hatten einen **ernsten** Unfall mit unserem alten Auto.	We had a ______________ accident with our old car.
11° Mia hatte einen **Bluterguss** im Gesicht, nachdem sie die Treppe hinuntergefallen war.	Mia had a ______________ on her face after she had fallen down the stairs.
12° Zum Glück hatte sie keine **Knochen**brüche.	Luckily she hadn't broken any ______________.
13° Er arbeitet als **Berater** im Krankenhaus.	He works as a ______________ at a hospital.

10 Word search

Finde 9 Wörter und übersetze sie.

M	A	T	E	D	B	A	R	G
R	Y	N	E	O	L	O	V	E
A	P	E	N	N	U	R	S	E
C	P	E	R	S	U	A	D	E
S	C	R	E	E	C	H	W	T

______________ ______________

______________ ______________

______________ ______________

______________ ______________

____

11 Find the right words

Setze die richtigen Wörter in die Sätze ein. Es gibt mehr Wörter, als du brauchst.

counsellor – damage – junction – paramedics – persuade – pulled up – rush – seriously – stretcher – supposed – take it easy – unconscious – walk

1 When it's late I always ______________ my girlfriend home.
2 An old car ______________ and some strange people got out.
3 We're trying to ______________ our parents to buy a dog.
4 What time are you ______________ to be home?
5 After a mile you'll come to a big ______________ where you have to turn left.
6 Smoking will ______________ your health.
7 When the ball hit his head he dropped down and was ______________ for a few seconds.
8 We called an ambulance and the ______________ took him to the hospital.
9 Fortunately he wasn't ______________ hurt.
10 But he was told to ______________ for a while.

New words ► *p. 45 | VOCABULARY pp. 225–226*

1 Die Französische **Revolution** begann 1789.	The French ______________ started in 1789.
2 Die Arbeiter verlangten höhere **Löhne**.	The workers demanded higher ______________.
3 Die Arbeits**bedingungen** müssen verbessert werden.	Working ______________ must be improved.
4 Bitte **behalte meine** Tasche im **Auge**, während ich uns einen Kaffee hole.	Please ______________ my bag while I'm getting us some coffee.
5 Ich versuche, keine Kleidung aus **Ausbeutungsbetrieben** zu kaufen.	I try not to buy clothes that were made in ______________.
6 Leon arbeitet in einer Schuh**fabrik**.	Leon works in a shoe ______________.
7 Ich finde es **unmöglich**, ein 4-jähriges Kind allein zu Hause zu lassen.	I think it's ______________ to leave a 4-year-old child at home on its own.
8 Dein T-Shirt ist **verkehrt herum**.	Your T-shirt is ______________.

New words ▸ *p. 46 | VOCABULARY p. 226*

1 Mein Vater ist **Ingenieur**.	My father is an ______________________.
2 Überall hängen **Werbeplakate**.	There are ______________________ everywhere.
3 Wer ist für die **Einstellung** neuer Mitarbeiter zuständig?	Who is in charge of the ______________________ of new staff?
4 Du musst jedes **Zitat** kennzeichnen.	You must mark each ______________________.
5 Ich hatte noch keine Zeit, Bilder in meiner neuen Wohnung **aufzuhängen**.	I haven't had time to ______________________ any pictures in my new flat.
6 Er **wirkte** in vielen Filmen **mit**.	He ______________________ in lots of films.
7 Ich habe mehrmals nachgefragt, aber noch keine Antwort **erhalten**.	I've asked a few times, but I haven't ______________________ an answer yet.
8 Großvater **ermutigte** mich, ein Instrument zu lernen.	Grandad ______________________ me to learn an instrument.
9 Wir haben zwei Kaninchen: ein **weibliches** und ein **männliches**.	We have two rabbits: one ______________________ and one ______________________.
10 Der Roman ist voller **Klischees** über Mädchen und Jungen.	The novel is full of ______________________ about girls and boys.
11 Leider gibt es immer noch Menschen, die Vorurteile gegen **Nichtweiße** haben.	Unfortunately there are still people with prejudices against ______________________.
12 Frauen sind immer noch in der **Minderheit** in Führungspositionen.	Women are still in the ______________________ in leading positions.
13 Nora studiert **Maschinenbau** in München.	Nora studies ______________________ in Munich.
14 Sie möchte in einer großen Firma **Karriere** machen.	She wants a ______________________ in a big company.
15 Alter und **Geschlecht** spielen immer noch eine große Rolle bei der Jobvergabe.	Age and ______________________ still play a big role when it comes to job opportunities.
16 Das ist **nahezu** alles, was ich über ihn weiß.	That's ______________________ everything I know about him.

12 Opposites

Finde das Gegenteil.

1 possible ◂▸ ______________________

2 minority ◂▸ ______________________

3 send ◂▸ ______________________

4 male ◂▸ ______________________

5 take sth. down ◂▸ ______________________

13 Lost words

Setze die richtigen Wörter in die Sätze ein.

1 We are raising money ______________ our partner school in South Africa.

2 Can you give me a lift ______________ town?

3 Please put the TV ______________. I want to watch the news.

4 We crashed ______________ a van on the way home.

5 In my first job I had a wage ______________ 2000 euros a month.

6 Keep an eye ______________ your bag at the station.

7 It's a quote ______________ a well-known book.

8 I haven't had time to put ______________ pictures in my new flat.

9 Jim will feature ______________ my next film.

10 I'm planning a career ______________ engineering.

11 Teachers ought to take a strong stand ______________ bullying.

12 Are you involved ______________ any social projects?

13 She pointed ______________ that smoking was very unhealthy.

14 Odd word out

Finde das Wort, das nicht in die Reihe passt.

1 engineer – nurse – counsellor – location

2 feature – wage – encourage – receive

3 receive – give – provide – spend

4 many – loads of – a lot – few

5 monument – democracy – minimum – siren

New words ▸ *p. 47 | VOCABULARY pp. 226–227*

1 Habt ihr einen schönen **Ort** für eure Feier gefunden?	Have you found a nice ______________ for your party?
2 Ich konnte der **Handlung** des Films nicht folgen.	I couldn't follow the ______________ of the film.
3 Wer hat das **Drehbuch** zum Film geschrieben?	Who wrote the ______________ for the film?
4 Bitte **rette** mich, es ist so langweilig hier.	Please ______________ me, it's so boring here.
5 Der Räuber trug eine orange Jacke, sodass man ihn leicht **erkennen** konnte.	The robber wore an orange jacket so that it was easy to ______________ him.

15 Plurals

Ergänze den Plural. Einmal gibt es zwei Möglichkeiten.

	Singular	Plural		Singular	Plural
1	giraffe		4	opportunity	
2	thief		5	ostrich	
3	national holiday		6	wage	

16 Word friends

In jedem Leuchtturm gibt es drei Wörter bzw. Wortverbindungen, die man direkt nach dem Verb in der Kuppel verwenden kann. Eines passt jeweils nicht. Streiche es durch.

New words MORE CHALLENGE ▸ *p. 52 | VOCABULARY p. 237*

1° Jeder in meiner Familie hat ein **Fahrrad**.	Everyone in my family has a ________________.
2° Ich möchte mich für mein **beschämendes** Verhalten entschuldigen.	I want to apologize for my ________________ behaviour.
3° Mein Bruder ist Arzt und ist sehr **wohlhabend**.	My brother is a doctor and is very ________________.
4° Ich möchte **Ihre Aufmerksamkeit auf** dieses schöne Bild **lenken**.	I'd like to ________________ this nice picture.
5° Als ich die quietschenden Reifen hörte, sprang ich **instinktiv** zur Seite.	When I heard the screeching tyres I jumped aside ________________.
6° Der Streit wurde immer aggressiver, bevor die Nachbarn **einschritten**.	The argument became very aggressive before the neighbours ________________.
7° Einige Schulen sind in einem sehr schlechten **Zustand**.	Some schools are in a very bad ________________.
8° Das Gewitter wurde zu einer **bedrohlichen** Gefahr für die Camper.	The storm became a ________________ danger for the campers.
9° Er **fluchte**, als ihm sein Handy ins Wasser fiel.	He ________________ when he dropped his mobile into the water.
10° Meine Eltern wohnen **weiter** die Straße hoch.	My parents live ________________ up the road.
11° **Warst** du **dabei**, als der Unfall geschah?	________________ you ________________ when the accident happened?
12° Ich bin **um** dein **Wohl besorgt**.	I'm ________________ your ________________.
13° Sie besitzt ein Auto und ein **Motorrad**.	She owns a car and a ________________.
14° Zeichne eine **gerade** Linie.	Draw a ________________ line

New words MORE CHALLENGE ▸ *pp. 52–53 | VOCABULARY p. 238*

1° Aus ihrem Alter **schloss** ich, dass sie noch Grundschülerin war.	From her age I ____________ that she was still a primary school student.
2° **Falls** er den Job **bekommt**, müsste er nach London umziehen.	____________ the job, he would have to move to London.
3° Ich hatte starke Kopfschmerzen und **zog** mich **zurück**.	I had a bad headache, so I ____________.
4° Dass wir uns verlaufen haben, ist **unerklärlich**.	It's ____________ that we got lost.
5° Wir meldeten den **Vorfall** der Polizei.	We reported the ____________ to the police.
6° Seit wir uns das letzte Mal gesehen haben, **ist** viel Zeit **vergangen**.	A lot of time ____________ since we last saw each other.
7° Er gab einen genauen **Bericht** über den Vorfall der letzten Nacht.	He gave a detailed ____________ of what happened last night.
8° Was liest du gern? – Jugendmagazine, Fanmagazine, **dergleichen**.	What do like reading? – Youth magazines, fan magazines, ____________.
9° Ich hatte große **Bedenken** gegen die Party.	I had great ____________ about the party.
10° Er **bereicherte** den Abend mit seiner Musik.	He ____________ the evening with his music.

17 Find the words

Trage die Wörter in das Rätselgitter ein. Sie enden alle auf -E.

1 say rude things
2 the physical or mental condition that a person is in
3 the safety and health of a person
5 believe sth. after you have heard or seen sth.
6 say sth. in a certain situation to change things for the better

④

					1				E
					2				E
			3						E
			4						E
		5							E
	6								E
7									E

⑦

18 Crossword

Hier kannst du testen, wie gut du die Vokabeln der Unit 2 behalten hast.

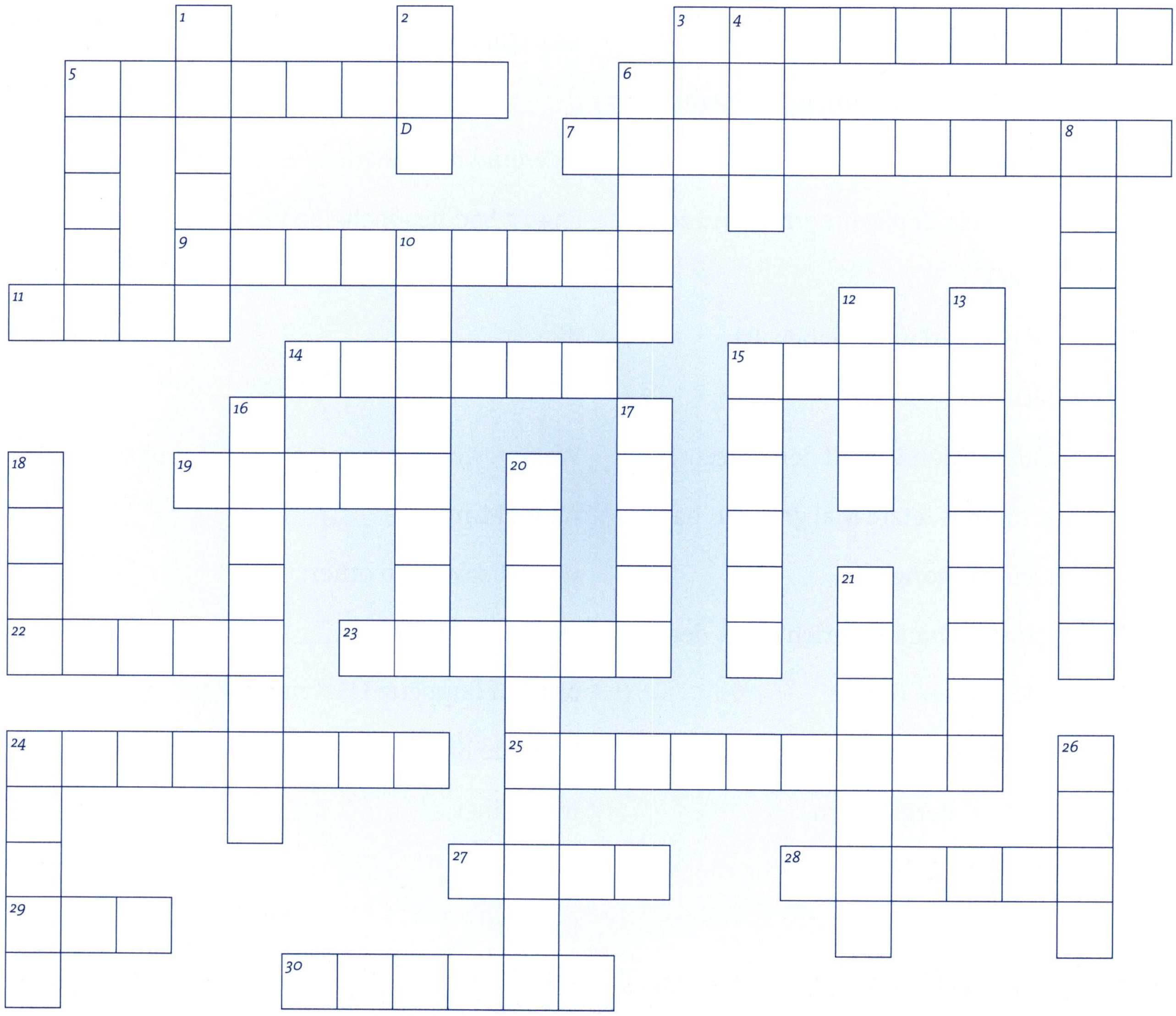

1 loben, rühmen
2 wahnsinnig, verrückt
3 Ausbeutungsbetrieb
4 Lohn, Gehalt
5 → (das) Überleben
5 ↓ Bühne
6 Sirene
7 Honigkuchen, Pfefferkuchen
8 hinterher, danach
9 Unterschrift
10 retuschieren, nachbessern
11 Internet-Mem, Internet-phänomen
12 männlich
13 Scheinwerfer(licht)
14 Karriere; Werdegang
15 → Verfolgung, Verfolgungsjagd
15 ↓ (er)schaffen, kreieren
16 vollständig
17 Zitat
18 Verbrennung, Brandverletzung
19 Macht, Kraft, Stärke
20 Politiker/in
21 Flüchtling
22 Roman
23 (Aus-)Wahl
24 → Politik
24 ↓ beweisen; nachweisen
25 unterbrechen
26 eine Ewigkeit
27 Mitfahrgelegenheit
28 weiblich
29 über, durch, per
30 fordern, verlangen

Future visions

New words ▸ *pp. 54–55 | VOCABULARY pp. 227–228*

1 Ich habe die **Vision**, einmal in New York zu arbeiten.	I have a ______________ of working in New York one day.
2 Er kann mithilfe eines **Exoskeletts** wieder ein paar Schritte machen.	He can do a few steps with the help of an ______________.
3 In diesem Test ist der **Gebrauch** von Wörterbüchern nicht erlaubt.	The ______________ of dictionaries is not allowed in this test.
4 Der Brand dauerte mehrere Stunden und ein **Feuerwehrmann** wurde verletzt.	The fire went on for hours and one ______________ was hurt.
5 Wir **liefern** auch am Sonntag.	We ______________ on Sundays too.
6 **Drohnen** können vielfach eingesetzt werden.	______________ can be used in many ways.
7 Oma hat mir ein **Päckchen** zum Geburtstag geschickt.	Grandma sent me a ______________ for my birthday.
8 Hast du deine **Medizin** genommen?	Have you taken your ______________?
9 Normalerweise trage ich **Kontaktlinsen**. Nur bei Wind setze ich meine Brille auf.	I usually wear ______________. When it's windy I wear glasses.
10 Letzte Woche ist bei uns der **Strom** für eine Stunde ausgefallen.	Last week we had a ______________ cut that lasted about an hour.
11 Ich bringe meinen Schlafsack und mein **Kissen** mit.	I'll bring my sleeping bag and my ______________.
12 Kürzlich hat es einen schweren Unfall mit einem **fahrerlosen** Fahrzeug gegeben.	There was a serious accident with a ______________ vehicle recently.
13 **Naturwissenschaftler** finden immer mehr über Mikroorganismen heraus.	______________ are discovering more and more facts about microorganisms.
14 Er ging **voraus**. Wir folgten ihm.	He walked ______________. We followed him.

1 Definitions

Welche Wörter werden hier gesucht?

1 Someone whose job it is to put out a fire: ____________________

2 Something you take when you're ill: ____________________

3 Something you put your head on in bed: ____________________

4 Someone who works in physics, biology or chemistry: ____________________

5 Something that flies without a pilot and is controlled from the ground: ____________________

New words

▸ *p. 56 | VOCABULARY p. 228*

1 Nur wenige Menschen tragen noch eine **Armbanduhr**. Die meisten lesen die Uhrzeit von ihrem Handy ab.	Few people wear a ____________________ these days. Most people check their mobile to tell the time.
2 In den meisten Museen darf man nichts **anfassen**.	In most museums you aren't allowed to ____________________ anything.
3 Sie entwirft **tragbare** Kleidung für viele Anlässe.	She designs ____________________ clothes for lots of occasions.
4 Das **Gerät** hilft mir beim Abnehmen.	This ____________ helps me to lose weight.
5 **Funkkopfhörer** sind eine wunderbare Erfindung.	____________________ are a wonderful invention.
6 Kannst du bitte diese schwere Tasche für mich **tragen**.	Can you please ____________________ this heavy bag for me.
7 Unser Lehrer schreibt Wichtiges immer an die **Tafel**.	Our teacher always writes important things on the ____________________.
8 Das Hotel hat einen großen **Fitnessraum**.	The hotel has a big ____________________.
9 Ich habe wichtige **Daten** verloren, als mir mein Laptop gestohlen wurde.	I lost important ____________________ when my laptop was stolen.
10 Nach einem Tag am Schreibtisch brauche ich **Bewegung**.	I need some ____________________ after a day at my desk.

2 *-less* or *-ful* or both?

Welche Wörter kannst du mit -less *zu einem neuen Wort verbinden, welche mit* -ful*? Einige der Wörter ergeben sowohl mit der Endung* -less *als auch mit der Endung* -ful *sinnvolle neue Wörter. Übersetze alle Wörter.*

	-less		-ful	
	careless	schlampig	careful	vorsichtig
1				
2				
3				
4				
5				
6				
7				
8				
9				
10				

New words ▸ *p. 57 | VOCABULARY p. 228*

1 Der Bus war voller Schüler und viele Telefone **summten**.	The bus was full of students and lots of phones ____________.
2 Der Kuchen ist lecker, aber ich kann ihn leider nicht **aufessen**.	The cake is delicious, but unfortunately I can't ____________ it.
3 Tom **stöhnte**, als er die vielen Hausaufgaben sah, die er erledigen musste.	Tom ____________ when he saw the amount of homework he had to do.
4 Mit einer **Datenbrille** kann man in virtuelle Welten eintauchen.	With a ____________ you can dive into virtual reality.

New words ▸ *pp. 58–59 | VOCABULARY p. 229*

1 Ich kann so nicht **weitermachen**.	I can't ____________ like this.
2 Wir benutzen nur Papier aus **nachhaltiger** Forstwirtschaft.	We only use paper from ____________ forestry.
3 Die Entwicklung verschiedener Technologien hat zum wirtschaftlichen **Wachstum** der westlichen Gesellschaften geführt.	The development of various technologies has led to economic ____________ in western societies.
4 Das **Mittelalter** dauerte ungefähr 1000 Jahre.	____________ lasted for about 1000 years.
5 Zurzeit leben etwa 7,4 **Milliarden** Menschen auf der Erde.	At present about 7.4 ____________ people live on earth.
6 **7000 v. Chr.**	____________
7 **1000 n. Chr.**	____________
8 Was sagt uns dieses **Diagramm**?	What does this ____________ tell us?
9 Warum bist du so **pessimistisch**? Du wirst bestimmt einen Job finden?	Why are you so ____________? I'm sure you'll find a job.
10 Mia war **optimistisch**, die Wohnung zu bekommen.	Mia was ____________ about getting the flat.
11 **Meiner Ansicht nach** werfen die Leute zu viel Essen weg.	____________ people throw away too much food.

3 Linking

Verbinde die richtigen deutschen und englischen Sätze miteinander.

1 He can keep the book if he likes.
2 Keep up the good work, Luka!
3 If you keep on like this, you'll get in trouble.
4 Where do you keep your books, Luka?
5 Keep away from trouble.
6 Keep me posted, please.
7 I asked him to be quiet, but he kept shouting at me.

A Wo bewahrst du deine Bücher auf, Luka?
B Wenn er möchte, kann er das Buch behalten.
C Ich bat ihn ruhig zu sein, aber er schrie mich weiter an.
D Halt dich von Streitereien fern.
E Mach weiter so, Luka!
F Halte mich bitte auf dem Laufenden.
G Wenn du so weitermachst, kriegst du Ärger.

New words ► p. 60 | VOCABULARY pp. 229–230

1 Deutschland hat **Grenzen** zu neun Ländern, darunter Polen, Österreich und Frankreich.	Germany has ______________ with nine countries, among them Poland, Austria and France.
2 Neue Technologien **faszinieren** mich.	New technologies ______________ me.
3 Das Theaterstück war ein großer **Erfolg**.	The play was a big ______________.
4 Glaubst du, dass es **Marsmenschen** gibt?	Do you believe in the existence of ______________?
5 Unser **Planet** ist die Erde.	Our ______________ is the Earth.
6 Segeln im Naturschutzgebiet ist eine sehr **umstrittene** Angelegenheit.	Sailing in a nature reserve is very ______________ matter.
7 Meine **Voraussage** ist, dass es bald verboten wird.	My ______________ is that it will be forbidden soon.
8 Ich versuche, **bis 20 Uhr** zu Hause zu sein.	I'll try to be home ______________.
9 Wir hatten große **Schwierigkeiten**, eine geeignete Wohnung zu finden.	We had great ______________ finding a suitable flat.
10 Lise Meitner war **Pionierin** der Kern-forschung.	Lise Meitner was a ______________ in nuclear research.
11 Er ist eher ein **Möchtegern**-Schauspieler als ein großer Künstler.	He is more of a ______________ actor than a great artist.
12 Ich **habe** mich **für** einen Spanischkurs **angemeldet**.	I ______________ a Spanish course.
13 Hör auf, Musik zu hören, und **konzentriere** dich auf deine Hausaufgaben.	Stop listening to music and ______________ your homework.

4 What are the words?

Setze das richtige Wort in die englischen Sätze ein.

1 She's ______________ a heavy box. She's ______________ a nice dress.

2 My PE teacher says I need more ______________. I couldn't do ______________ 5 and 6.

3 The film ______________ an hour ago. Sorry, I can't ______________ the soup.

5 Numbers and letters

Zu jeder Zahl gehört ein Buchstabe. Finde zuerst die Lösungswörter. Vervollständige dann den Lösungssatz.

Hi Grandad,

Thank you for the P A R C E L [1 2 3 4 5 6] you sent me for my birthday. Had Mum told you that I wanted a _ _ _ _ _ [7 3 8 9 5]? It's _ _ _ _ _ _ _ _ _ [10 8 9 7 5 3 11 12 6]! I can fix my phone to it and take photos _ _ _ _ _ [2 13 8 14 5] the clouds – when they're hanging _ _ _ [6 8 10]. Later I can put my phone in my _ _ _ _ - _ _ _ _ _ _ _ [15 5 2 7 - 16 8 12 9 18 5 7] _ _ _ _ _ _ _ [7 19 20 1 6 2 24] and watch things you can't see from the ground. I can hear you _ _ _ _ _ [22 3 8 2 9], Grandad ☺. But it's fun and I _ _ _ _ _ [20 1 5 9 7] a lot of time outside and get a lot of _ _ _ _ _ _ _ _ [5 23 5 3 4 19 20 5].

I've always been _ _ _ _ _ _ _ _ _ _ [11 2 20 4 19 9 2 18 5 7] by new technical gadgets, and I think _ _ _ _ _ _ [7 3 8 9 8 20] can be _ _ _ _ _ _ [12 20 5 11 12 6] in many different _ _ _ _ [10 2 24 20]. They can _ _ _ _ _ _ _ [7 5 6 19 14 5 3] things from the _ _ _ _ _ _ _ _ [16 2 19 9 6 2 9 7] to small islands or bring _ _ _ _ _ _ _ _ [16 5 7 19 4 19 9 5] to people who live in remote areas.

When are you coming to see us?

I can't _ _ _ _ [10 2 19 18] _ _ [18 8] _ _ _ _ [20 15 8 10] _ _ _ [24 8 12] _ _ _ [2 6 6] _ _ [16 24] _ _ _ [9 5 10] _ _ _ _ _ _ [1 15 8 18 8 20].

Love,

Molly

New words

▸ p. 61 | VOCABULARY p. 230

1 Ich wollte um Fünf zu Hause sein, **schaffte** es aber nicht.	I wanted to be home at 5 pm, but I didn't ____________.
2 Zu meiner Abschlussfeier werde ich einen **Anzug** tragen.	I'll wear a ____________ for my graduation.
3 Wir hatten eine **wunderbare** Zeit in London.	We had a ____________ time in London.
4 Mark singt im **Chor**.	Mark sings in a ____________.

6 Bits and pieces

Verbinde die Silben, um englische Wörter zu bilden. Übersetze diese dann ins Deutsche.

1 de	cess	__________	__________
2 driver	able	__________	__________
3 opti	cise	__________	__________
4 fire	liver	__________	__________
5 wear	less	__________	__________
6 exer	vice	__________	__________
7 de	mistic	__________	__________
8 sustain	mistic	__________	__________
9 pessi	fighter	__________	__________
10 suc	able	__________	__________

New words ► p. 62 | VOCABULARY pp. 230–231

1 Ich dachte, du würdest die Wohnung putzen, aber das war wohl **Wunschdenken**.	I thought you'd clean the flat, but that was just __________.
2 Sie haben Ihr **Reiseziel** erreicht.	You have reached your __________.
3 Wir haben **einige** Monate im Ausland gearbeitet.	We worked abroad for __________ months.
4 Ich finde es spannend, Städte alleine zu **erkunden**.	I think it's exciting to __________ cities on my own.
5 Max hatte mich auf seine Party eingeladen, aber **leider** hatte ich keine Zeit.	Max had invited me to his party, but __________ I had no time to go.

7 What's the right word?

Kreise das Wort ein, das in den Satz passt.

1 He thought he'd get the job, but that was just wishful thinking / wishing thoughts / wishful thought.

2 John has sung in lots of choruses / chors / choirs.

3 I've signed in / signed up / signed for a Spanish class.

4 The data was / were / are collected over the last five years.

5 Although life wasn't always easy for my mother, she was usually very optimist / optimistic / optimism.

6 The graph shows you how much house prices have rised / risen / rosed in the last three years.

8 Word labyrinth

Übersetze die Wörter ins Englische. Trage die englischen Wörter in das Labyrinth ein. Die Anfangsbuchstaben helfen dir. Das Lösungswort findest du in den blauen Feldern.

unglücklicherweise, leider – erforschen, erkunden – mehrere, einige – sehr schön, wunderbar – Anzug, Kostüm – kontrovers, umstritten – n. Chr. – Vorhersage, Voraussage – Wachstum

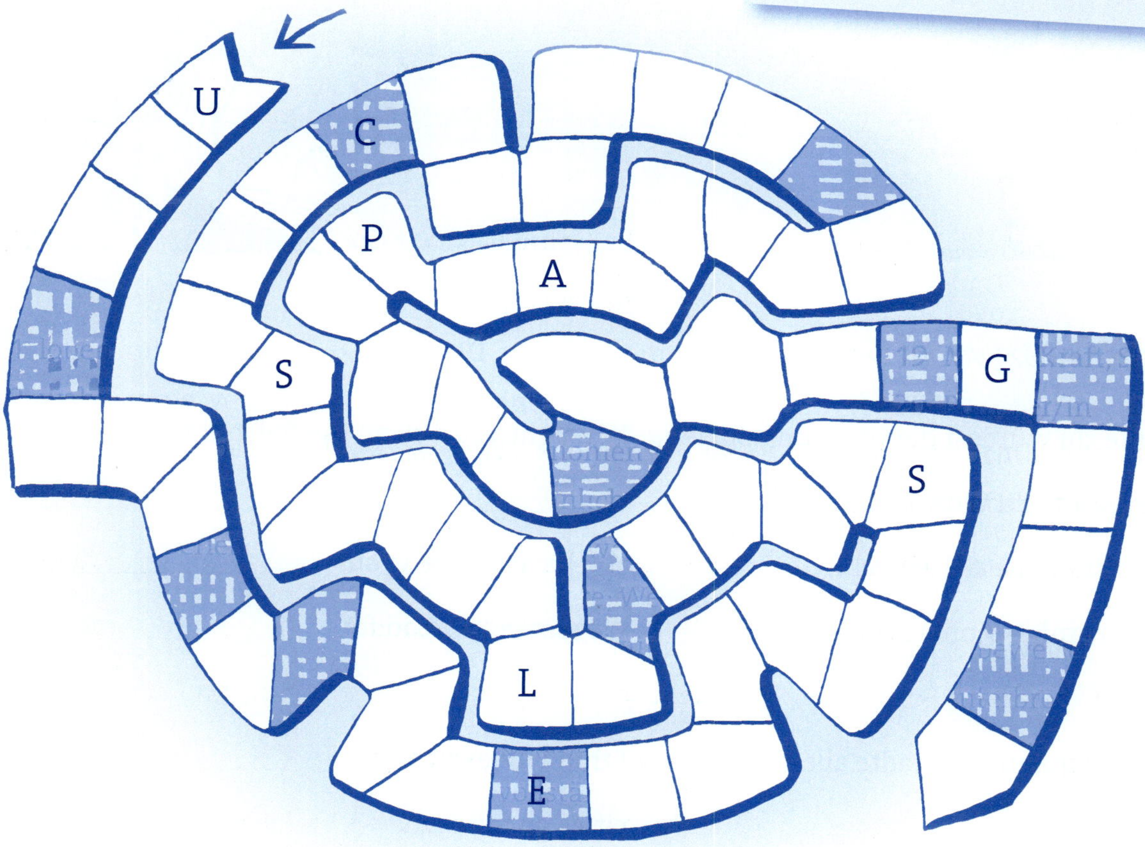

Lösungswort: ______________________

New words ► *p. 63 and pp. 130–131 | VOCABULARY pp. 231–232*

1 Die **Erderwärmung** hat in den letzten Jahren deutlich zugenommen.	______ has clearly increased over the last years.
2 Weißt du, wer den Schaden an meinem Auto **verursacht** hat?	Do you know who ______ the damage to my car?
3 Die Hauspreise werden weiter **steigen**.	House prices will continue to ______.
4 Ich habe **aus Versehen** alle Daten gelöscht.	I have deleted all my data ______.
5 Es gab nur **wenig** Auswahl auf der Speisekarte.	There was ______ choice on the menu.
6 Die Insel ist mit einer Brücke mit dem **Festland** verbunden.	The island is connected with the ______ by a bridge.
7 Wir haben den Kuchen **allein** gebacken.	We've made the cake ______.
8 Ein **Mob** von zwanzig Betrunkenen wollte in den Bus steigen.	A ______ of twenty drunken people wanted to get on the bus.
9 Du kannst dein Fahrrad in den **Schuppen** stellen.	You can put your bike in the ______.
10 In vielen Dörfern liegt der **Friedhof** hinter der Kirche.	In many villages the ______ lies behind the church.
11 Sie kam **keuchend** die Treppe hoch.	She climbed the stairs ______ing for breath.

9 What are the right words: *little – a little – few – a few*?

Setze die richtigen Wörter in die Sätze ein.

1 We didn't go on holiday when I was a child because we had very ______ money.

2 ______ people will ever be able to fly to the moon.

3 May I ask you ______ questions?

4 Gran gives me ______ pocket money each week.

5 ______ people have offered to help us move, but we still need more.

New words ▸ *pp. 64–65 and pp. 130–131 | VOCABULARY pp. 232–233*

1 Viele Leute haben **Angst vor** dem Fliegen.	Lots of people have a ______________ flying.
2 Eine große **Menschenmenge** wartete vor dem Kinoeingang.	A huge ______________ was waiting in front of the cinema entrance.
3 Wir **ruderten** zur Insel.	We ______________ to the island.
4 Ich habe eine Landkarte dabei, **falls** wir uns verlaufen.	I've brought a map, ______________ we get lost.
5 Ich würde gern ein **Bad** nehmen.	I'd like to take a ______________.
6 Ich kann nicht **rückwärts**fahren.	I can't drive ______________.
7 **So macht man das.**	______________
8 Ich kann nur nach **vorn schauend** Bus fahren, sonst wird mir **schwindelig**.	I can only ride on buses ______________. Otherwise I feel ______________.
9 Bitte **pustet** alle Kerzen aus, bevor ihr ins Bett geht.	Please ______________ out all the candles before you go to bed.
10 Er hatte seit vielen Stunden nichts gegessen und fühlte sich **schwach**.	He hadn't eaten anything for hours and felt ______________.
11 Wer ist der **Erzähler** in der Geschichte?	Who is the ______________ of the story?
12 Wir haben eine **Flaschenpost** am Strand gefunden.	We found a ______________ on the beach.

10 One German word – different English words

Das deutsche Wort „man" wird im Englischen unterschiedlich übersetzt. Setze mögliche Wörter in die englischen Sätze ein.

1 Man sollte nie ohne gültige Fahrkarte in einen Zug steigen.

______________ should never get on a train without a valid ticket.

2 Man sagt, englisches Essen sei schlecht, aber das ist falsch.

______________ say English food is bad, but that's wrong.

3 Man sagt, unsere neuen Nachbarn seien komisch.

______________ say our new neighbours are strange.

11 Opposites

Finde das Gegenteil.

1 begin	◄►	______________	4 forwards	◄►	______________
2 optimistic	◄►	______________	5 more time	◄►	______________
3 stop doing sth.	◄►	______________	6 island	◄►	______________

New words

► *pp. 63–64 | VOCABULARY pp. 233–234*

! *Wenn du den Text auf den Seiten 63 und 64 in deinem Schülerbuch gelesen und die zusätzlichen Wörter daraus gelernt hast, kannst du diese* ***New words*** *bearbeiten.*

1° Nach dem Sturm waren die Straßen **menschenleer**.	After the storm, the streets were ______________.
2° Einige Hausbesetzer waren in das **verfallene** Haus gezogen.	Some squatters had moved into the ______________ house.
3° Setz dich nicht auf den Ball. Er könnte **platzen**.	Don't sit on the ball. It might ______________.
4° Bitte **werde langsamer**. Die Straße ist sehr eng.	Please ______________. The road is very narrow.
5° Wenn wir die Reise wieder **verschieben**, fahren wir vielleicht nie.	If we ______________ the trip again, we might never do it.
6° Sam war ein **winziges** Baby.	Sam was a ______________ baby.
7° Mein Onkel ist ein **Einzelgänger**. Er kommt nie zu Familienfeiern.	My uncle is a ______________. He never attends family celebrations.
8° Am Wochenende **hänge** ich meistens mit Freunden **herum**.	I usually ______________ with friends at the weekend.
9° Ich wusste nie, **wem** ich trauen konnte.	I never knew ______________ I could trust.
10° Ich bin auf einem Stein **ausgerutscht** und habe mir den Arm gebrochen.	I ______________ on a stone and broke my arm.
11° Die Kekse könnten Nüsse **enthalten**.	The biscuits may ______________ nuts.

New words ▸ p. 64 | VOCABULARY pp. 234–235

! *Wenn du den Text auf Seite 64 in deinem Schülerbuch gelesen und die zusätzlichen Wörter daraus gelernt hast, kannst du die* ***New words und Aufgabe 12*** *und* ***13*** *bearbeiten.*

1° Die Kinder **stürmten** zum Spielplatz.	The children ______________ towards the playground.
2° Regen **platschte** auf das Dach.	Rain ______________ onto the roof.
3° Sie war sehr müde und **schleppte** sich die Treppe hinauf.	She was very tired and ______________ herself up the stairs.
4° Wir kamen an einen schönen See und setzten uns ans **Ufer**.	We arrived at a nice lake and sat down at its ______________.
5° Unser Gemüse**vorrat** ist nicht sehr groß.	Our vegetable ______________ isn't very big.
6° Er **machte** eine **Pause**, um etwas Wasser zu trinken, bevor er weitersprach.	He ______________ to drink some water, then continued to speak.
7° Mir geht der **Atem** aus.	I'm running out of ______________.
8° Sie **besitzen** mehrere Häuser.	They ______________ several houses.
9° Das Fahrrad **gehört** Hülya.	The bike ______________ Hülya.
10° Als wir Kinder waren, **aßen wir immer** mit der ganzen Familie.	When we were children ______________ with the whole family.
11° Wie durch **Zauberei** habe ich meinen Schlüssel im Sand wiedergefunden.	As if by ______________ I found my key in the sand.
12° Wir hatten jegliches Zeit**gefühl** verloren.	We'd lost any ______________ time.
13° Die Sonne **knallte** auf uns **herunter**.	The sun ______________ on us.
14° Er **ließ** die letzten Wochen mit seiner Freundin **noch einmal Revue passieren**.	He ______________ the last weeks with his girlfriend.
15° Eine Bootsfahrt bei Gewitter – welch ein **Albtraum**!	A boat trip in a storm – what a ______________!

12 Word snake

Übersetze die Verben in der Schlange und trage ihren Infinitiv sowie das simple past und das past participle in die Liste ein.

	Infinitive	Simple past	Past participle
1			
2			
3			
4			
5			

13 What are the words: *in*, *off*, *on* or *up*?

Setze die richtige Präposition in die Sätze ein. Achte auf die Bedeutung.

1 I want to put __________ some photos in my bedroom. Could you help me?

2 Sam always puts __________ his homework. I don't know what to do with him.

3 Where shall I put __________ my name?

4 Put __________ some warm clothes. It's cold outside.

New words ▸ *p. 66 | VOCABULARY p. 235*

1 Unsere Nachbarn haben einen **Roboter**, der den Rasen mäht.	Our neighbours have a __________________ that cuts the grass.
2 In Hannover gab es im Jahr 2000 eine Welt**ausstellung**.	There was a world __________________ in Hanover in the year 2000.
3 Hier kannst du Obst, Gemüse, Eier **und so weiter** kaufen.	Here you can buy fruit, vegetables, eggs __________________________.
4 Das Smartphone ist ein sehr nützliches **Gerät**.	The smartphone is a very useful __________.
5 Ich kann **ohne** Fernsehen **auskommen**.	I can __________________ television.
6 Sie zeigte mir ihre **Zeichnung**.	She showed me her ______________.

New words ▸ *pp. 67–69* | *VOCABULARY pp. 235–236*

1 Das Hotelzimmer war sehr schmutzig. Wir brachten eine **Beschwerde** beim Besitzer vor.	The hotel room was very dirty. We made a ____________ to the owner.
2 Dieser Stuhl ist sehr **unbequem**.	This chair is very ____________.
3 Bitte **zieh** deine Schuhe in der Wohnung **aus**.	Please ____________ your shoes in the flat.
4 Ich brauche eine **Batterie** für meine Kamera.	I need a ____________ for my camera.
5 Bei dem **schwachen** Licht kann ich nicht lesen.	I can't read in this ____________ light.
6 Das Hotel war weit weg vom Strand. **Außerdem** war das Essen schlecht.	The hotel was far away from the beach. ____________, the food was bad.
7 Wir **sollen** unsere Fahrräder **nicht** im Hausflur abstellen.	We're ____________ leave our bikes in the hall.
8 Mein kleiner Cousin kann von 1–100 **zählen**.	My little cousin can ____________ from 1–100.
9 Die Zahlen sind nicht sehr **akkurat**.	The figures aren't very ____________.
10 Die **Umstände**, in denen viele Flüchtlinge leben, sind erschreckend.	The ____________ in which a lot of refugees have to live are frightening.
11 Wenn Sie mit dem Gerät nicht zufrieden sind, bekommen Sie eine **Kostenerstattung**.	If you're not happy with the gadget, you will get a ____________.
12 Bitte **fügen** Sie ein Foto **bei**.	Please ____________ a photo.
13 Hier sind Ihr Wechselgeld und Ihre **Quittung**.	Here's your change and your ____________.
14 Wir müssen die Wohnung **innerhalb** der nächsten drei Wochen verlassen.	We have to leave the flat ____________ the next three weeks.
15 Ihre Beziehung **hielt** fünf Jahre.	Their relationship ____________ five years.
16 Ich habe nur eine **vage** Vorstellung davon, wie wir von hier nach Dortmund kommen.	I only have a ____________ idea how we'll get from here to Dortmund.
17 Ich habe einen **förmlichen** Brief an meinen Chef geschrieben.	I wrote a ____________ letter to my boss.
18 Dem Blitz folgte ein lauter **Donner**.	The flash was followed by loud ____________.

14 Definitions

Welche Wörter werden hier gesucht?

1 It's often preceded by a flash: ____________________

2 A piece of paper you get when you have bought something: ____________________

3 Money that is paid back to you: ____________________

4 Another word for "exact": ____________________

5 Think or say numbers one after the other in the right order: ____________________

6 Saying that you do not like something: ____________________

7 A picture you do with a pencil: ____________________

8 Another word for "device": ____________________

9 A group of things that are shown at a public place to a group of people: ____________________

10 A machine that can be programmed to do certain things: ____________________

New words MORE CHALLENGE ▸ *pp. 74–75 | VOCABULARY p. 238*

1° Eine **Mitschülerin** half mir bei Mathe.	A ____________________ helped me with maths.
2° Du solltest deinen Freund nicht vor allen Leuten **in Verlegenheit bringen**.	You shouldn't ____________________ your friend in front of all these people.
3° Unsere Englischlehrerin hat viel **Humor**.	Our English teacher has a great sense of ____________________.
4° Die Bank **wurde** zum zweiten Mal **ausgeraubt**.	The bank ____________________ for the second time.
5° Sam ist unser **Klassensprecher**.	Sam is our ____________________.
6° Mein Großvater **hielt eine Rede**, als mein Bruder heiratete.	My grandfather ____________________ when my brother got married.
7° Ich verstehe diesen **Ausdruck** nicht. Kannst du ihn mir erklären?	I don't understand this ____________________. Can you explain it to me?
8° Ich **habe** mir die Hausaufgaben **von** meinem Bruder **machen lassen**.	I ____________________ my homework ____________________ my brother.

16 Crossword

Hier kannst du testen, wie gut du die Vokabeln der Unit 3 behalten hast.

1 Gebrauch, Verwendung
2 Kopfkissen
3 wenig
4 Donner
5 mehrere, einige
6 Furcht, Angst
7 (Natur-)Wissenschaftler/in
8 Bewegung, Training
9 rückwärts; nach hinten
10 tragen; befördern
11 tragbar (Kleidung)
12 → Energie, Strom
12 ↓ Paket, Päckchen
13 Armbanduhr
14 (an)steigen
15 rudern
16 Bad; Badewanne
17 Kopfhörer
18 Fitnessraum; Fitnessstudio
19 Schwierigkeit(en)
20 Erzähler/in
21 → Friedhof
21 ↓ Diagramm, Kurve
22 (aus)liefern
23 schlecht, schwach
24 Gerät, Apparat
25 etw. aufessen; aufbrauchen
26 erforschen; erkunden
27 etw. bewirken, verursachen
28 berühren, anfassen
29 Anzug, Kostüm
30 Daten
31 nachhaltig, umweltverträglich

17 Word search

Hier kannst du testen, wie gut du die Vokabeln aus Band 6 behalten hast. Kreise 30 Wörter in dem Gitter ein. Die Fotos und die Bilderrahmen helfen dir. Du musst in 8 Richtungen suchen (→ ← ↓ ↑ ↖ ↗ ↘ ↙).

W	C	O	L	O	U	R	F	U	L	E	L	P	O	E	P
M	I	C	R	A	S	H	E	T	A	G	E	R	G	E	S
U	T	L	U	O	S	T	R	I	C	H	A	X	B	Y	D
L	R	S	D	R	W	A	L	L	E	T	C	Y	T	A	H
T	O	U	R	L	R	E	C	E	I	V	E	I	M	T	C
I	L	C	O	D	I	E	W	E	S	E	R	M	W	C	H
L	L	C	N	A	V	F	N	H	F	O	L	O	G	H	O
I	E	E	E	H	H	E	E	C	N	I	R	D	J	A	I
N	U	S	K	E	G	D	S	I	Y	G	Y	M	E	S	R
G	Q	S	L	A	M	U	M	N	B	O	A	R	D	E	O
U	I	P	T	D	I	Q	R	F	A	C	T	O	R	Y	N
A	N	S	Y	T	I	N	U	T	R	O	P	P	O	S	T
L	U	L	I	F	T	F	R	O	N	T	I	E	R	U	V

Scrambled words in English

ourfcolul – dliwilfe – regsegate – rtunitoppoy – schae – orminity – amd – eaahd – ontfrier

Words in German

Währung – mehrsprachig – einzigartig – Volk – Bühne – Mitfahrgelegenheit – Unfall, Zusammenstoß – erhalten – Wachstum – Erfolg

English G

Lighthouse 6 Wordmaster

Erarbeitet von:
Ursula Fleischhauer, Hannover

In Zusammenarbeit mit der Englischredaktion:
Klaus Unger (Projektleitung) und Eleanor Toal

Illustrationen:
Dorina Tessmann, Berlin

Cover Illustration:
Dorina Tessmann, Berlin

Layoutkonzept:
Klein & Halm Grafikdesign, Berlin

Umschlaggestaltung:
Cornelsen Verlag Design unter Verwendung der Entwürfe von Klein & Halm Grafikdesign, Berlin und kleiner & bold, Berlin

Layout und technische Umsetzung:
Andrea Päch (MeGA 14), Berlin

Fotos:
Fotolia (S. 7 Bild 1 (u. S. 20): rh2010, Bild 2 (u. S. 20): Anatoly Maslennikov, Bild 4 (u. S. 20): Valerii Kaliuzhnii, Bild 5 (u. S. 20 u. S. 55): connel_design; S. 16 Bild 4 (u. S. 20): goir, Bild 10 (u. S. 20 u. S. 55): bluebat; S. 20 2. v. oben re.: Bene Images; S. 37 Bild 4: Apart Foto; S. 55 Nadel: stalkerstudent, Chor: shin28, Tafel: 3dmavr, Sportraum: virtua73); **Shutterstock** (S. 16 Bild 8: Eric Isselee; S. 37 Bild 7: annet999; S. 55 Hütte: tektur, Puppe: Elena Noeva, Fabrik: Blablo101, Drohne: Slavoljub Pantelic, Anzug: Karkas)

www.cornelsen.de

1. Auflage, 1. Druck 2017

Alle Drucke dieser Auflage sind inhaltlich unverändert und können im Unterricht nebeneinander verwendet werden.

Druck: H. Heenemann, Berlin

ISBN 978-3-06-032569-6

Inhalt gedruckt auf säurefreiem Papier aus nachhaltiger Forstwirtschaft.

ENGLISH G

6

LIGHTHOUSE

Wordmaster
Lösungen

Cornelsen

Unit 1: Embrace diversity

New words p. 10
1 embrace 2 diversity 3 multicultural
4 rainbows 5 colonized 6 Diamonds 7 mix
8 religions 9 colourful 10 wildlife 11 low
12 currency

1 Find the right words
1 diversity = Vielfalt – diverse = vielfältig
2 culture = Kultur – cultural = kulturell
3 religion = Religion – religious = religiös

New words p. 11
1 apartheid 2 were segregated 3 public
4 system 5 was released 6 multilingual

2 Find the right words
1 colony = Kolonie – colonize = kolonisieren
2 segregation = Trennung – segregate = trennen
3 release = Freilassung, Befreiung – release = freilassen, befreien

3 Lost words
1 from 2 of 3 in, between 4 at 5 against

New words pp. 12–13
1 (back) then 2 elected, to be 3 memory of
4 access 5 poverty 6 Unemployment 7 suburb
8 Bakers 9 relationship 10 totally 11 dated
12 opportunity 13 documented 14 political
15 national holiday

4 What's the word: *chance, opportunity, possibility* or *way*?
1 opportunity/chance 2 possibility 3 ways
4 chance/opportunity

New words p. 14
1 in the wild 2 in spite of 3 unique
4 informative 5 conservation 6 step 7 edge
8 platform 9 ostrich 10 truly 11 weighs
12 aimed 13 effective

New words p. 15
1 rather than 2 advance 3 reply 4 preferable
5 insight 6 humans 7 creature

5 What are the words?
1 baker 2 diamond 3 rainbow 4 ostrich
5 platform 6 public 7 reply

Lösungswort: *embrace*

6 How do you say the words?
Betonung auf der 1. Silbe: creature diamond document public system

Betonung auf der 2. Silbe: diversity effective informative political relationship

New words p. 16
1 instead of 2 confused 3 In fact 4 majority
5 century 6 lingua franca

7 What's the right word?
1 currency 2 released 3 apartheid 4 rather than
5 insight 6 preferable

New words pp. 17–18
1 permanent 2 question mark 3 typical of
4 false friends

8 What's the right word?
1 prefer, to 2 instead of 3 preferably 4 instead
5 preferable to

9 What is it?
1 exclamation mark, Ausrufezeichen 2 hyphen, Bindestrich 3 colon, Doppelpunkt 4 question mark, Fragezeichen 5 comma, Komma 6 full stop, Punkt

New words p. 19
1 take care of 2 don't need, any more 3 return
4 crowded 5 shop window 6 frightened
7 a two-bedroomed flat 8 council flat 9 above
10 somehow

10 What'are the right words?
1 frightens 2 frightened of 3 frightening
4 frightened, frightening 5 frightening

New words pp. 20–21
1 heat, microwave 2 make yourself comfortable
3 people 4 have made a decision 5 silent 6 was about 7 From now on 8 passport 9 hugged
10 characterization 11 Characterize 12 response

11 Opposites
1 low 2 above 3 unemployment 4 majority

New words p. 19
1° tunnel 2° was covered 3° sudden 4° glimpse
5° echoed 6° hurry 7° every now and again
8° certainly 9° and neither did I 10° gulped down
11° straight 12° cartons

New words pp. 20–21
1° leftover 2° had turned yellow 3° olives
4° Pineapples 5° drifted 6° sighed 7° ring
8° pale 9° besides 10° dirty 11° dishes
12° dustbin 13° struggling 14° fear 15° turned away 16° streamed 17° was shaking
18° financial difficulties 19° talk, over with you
20° terror 21° Where, anyway

New words p. 21
1° and off we went to 2° bits 3° television 4° Do they even have streets? 5° forever

12 Word labyrinth
sigh – pale – dirty – dustbin – fear – hurry – certainly – cover – besides – difficulty – struggle

Lösungswort: *sudden*

New words p. 22
1 giraffe, giraffe/giraffes 2 fill in 3 gaps 4 Wi-fi
5 Check-in 6 facilities 7 thief, thieves
8 operating 9 unattended 10 remove
11 immediately 12 may

13 Scrambled words
1 thieves 2 unattended 3 immediately
4 facilities

New words p. 23
1 wallet 2 miss(ing) 3 ID/identification
4 student card 5 report

14 Crossword
1 poverty 2 operate 3 edge 4 microwave
5 silent 6 weigh 7 truly 8 giraffe 9 response
10 wallet 11 → century 11 ↓ creature 12 gap
13 confused 14 remove 15 step 16 elect
17 low 18 effective

New words pp. 24–25
1 mediation 2 historical 3 monument 4 provide
5 daily 6 minimum 7 translate 8 Some day
9 reaction 10 stick, mind 11 technique
12 voice-over 13 close-ups 14 medium shot
15 shot 16 long shot 17 swap

15 Bits and pieces
1 medium shot = Halbtotale
2 close-up = Nahaufnahme
3 prime minister = Premierminister/in
4 long shot = Totale
5 take place = stattfinden
6 voice-over = Off-Stimme, (Film-)Kommentar
7 some day = eines Tages
8 news item = Nachrichtenmeldung, Pressemeldung
9 student card = Schülerausweis, Studentenausweis
10 care about = wichtig nehmen

16 First letter – last letter
1 embrace 2 elect 3 typical 4 low 5 weigh
6 hug 7 giraffes 8 swap 9 provide 10 effective
11 edge 12 echo 13 opportunity

New words MORE CHALLENGE p. 30
1° Poach(ing) 2° at record levels 3° consequence
4° Certain 5° extinction 6° anti- 7° moon
8° hunt 9° surrounded 10° track 11° Armed
12° confronted 13° puts 14° Therefore 15° at a time 16° despite

17 Word search

A	B	C	D	D	E	F	G	H	W	N	R	U	T	E	R
I	J	T	R	A	N	S	L	A	T	E	K	L	M	N	O
P	Q	R	M	I	N	D	L	S	R	A	I	N	B	O	W
M	T	U	V	L	W	L	T	E	C	H	N	I	Q	U	E
I	E	T	X	Y	E	Z	A	P	R	O	V	I	D	E	P
N	C	D	N	T	E	S	I	L	E	N	T	F	P	W	A
I	C	H	I	E	D	B	A	K	E	R	D	L	M	I	S
M	U	I	F	A	M	G	H	K	I	I	A	W	E	L	S
U	R	S	P	C	T	U	C	J	A	T	K	E	M	D	P
M	R	T	E	C	L	I	N	M	F	M	N	I	O	L	O
O	E	O	O	E	T	P	O	O	Q	R	S	G	R	I	R
T	N	R	P	S	U	N	R	N	M	V	W	H	Y	F	T
X	C	I	L	S	D	M	I	C	R	O	W	A	V	E	Y
Z	Y	C	E	H	C	I	R	T	S	O	E	D	G	E	A
C	H	A	R	A	C	T	E	R	I	Z	A	T	I	O	N
C	I	L	B	U	P	A	S	U	B	U	R	B	X	B	C

Unit 2: Take a stand

New words pp. 32–33
1 take a stand against 2 creates

New words p. 34
1 activism 2 demonstration 3 protest 4 These days 5 airbrush 6 petition 7 signatures 8 power 9 estimate 10 get involved in 11 Memes

New words p. 34
1 pointed out 2 via 3 trolls, hurtful 4 loads of

New words p. 35
1 complete 2 solve the problem

1 Find the words
1 loads of 2 meme 3 estimate 4 protest 5 signature 6 solve 7 petition 8 hurtful 9 via 10 create 11 airbrush 12 power 13 point out

Lösungswort: *demonstration*

New words pp. 36–37
1 care about 2 chancellor 3 prime minister 4 politics 5 pay attention to 6 pension 7 ages 8 what politics is about 9 prove 10 choice 11 have a say in 12 democracy 13 politician

2 Word building
act = handeln; activism = Aktivismus

protest = protestieren;
protest = Protest(demonstration)

sign = unterschreiben; signature = Unterschrift

complete = vervollständigen; completion = Vervollständigung

choose = (aus)wählen; choice = (Aus-)Wahl

New words p. 38
1 robber 2 demanded 3 praised 4 came across 5 refugees 6 survival, remarkable 7 stage 8 news item 9 performers 10 interrupt

3 Linking
1 E 2 C 3 F 4 A 5 B 6 D

4 Lost words
1 out, in 2 of 3 about 4 to 5 in 6 across 7 to

5 Definitions
1 pension 2 prove 3 democracy 4 politician
5 robber 6 refugee

New words pp. 39–40
1 was, in progress 2 take place 3 rais(ing) money
4 wonderful 5 gingerbread 6 delicious
7 comparison 8 afterwards

6 Word ladder
1 date 2 late 3 hate 4 gate 5 game 6 came
7 care 8 card

New words pp. 41–43
1 forever/for ever 2 novel 3 Needle 4 com(ing), way 5 Headlights 6 lift 7 mad 8 chase 9 cops
10 Put, on 11 sirens 12 Flash 13 crash
14 crashed into 15 explosion 16 burns
17 alarmed 18 over time 19 Joyriding
20 I changed my mind

7 Word web
1 unique 2 people 3 remove 4 create 5 choice
6 praise 7 needle

8 Word pairs
1 get involved in 2 point sth. out 3 solve a problem 4 pay attention 5 put on the radio
6 crash into a car 7 change one's mind 8 be in progress 9 raise money

9 Word labyrinth
delicious – remarkable – wonderful – hurtful – complete – unattended – political – silent

Lösungswort: *confused*

New words p. 41
1° headed 2° walk, to 3° cut through 4° housing estate 5° high-rise building

New words pp. 41–42
1° screech 2° approached 3° The headlights were on full beam. 4° pulled up 5° persuade 6° furious
7° I'm, supposed to 8° speeding 9° speed hump
10° mates 11° scar 12° put his foot down
13° Right behind 14° junction 15° straight
16° damaged 17° unconscious

New words pp. 42–43
1° bloody 2° grabbed 3° paramedics, stretcher
4° rushed, to 5° sleepless 6° love 7° Take it easy
8° Lie back 9° nurse 10° serious 11° bruise
12° bones 13° counsellor

10 Word search

M	A	T	E	D	B	A	R	G
R	Y	N	E	O	L	O	V	E
A	P	E	N	N	U	R	S	E
C	P	E	R	S	U	A	D	E
S	C	R	E	E	C	H	W	T

1 mate = Freund/in, Kumpel
2 grab = packen, greifen (nach)
3 love = hier: Liebling
4 nurse = (Kranken-)Pfleger/in
5 persuade = überreden, überzeugen
6 screech = kreischen, quietschen
7 speed = rasen
8 scar = Narbe
9 bone = Knochen

11 Find the right words
1 walk 2 pulled up 3 persuade 4 supposed
5 junction 6 damage 7 unconscious
8 paramedics 9 seriously 10 take it easy

New words p. 45
1 Revolution 2 wages 3 conditions 4 keep an eye on 5 sweatshops 6 factory 7 impossible
8 inside out

New words p. 46
1 engineer 2 billboards 3 recruitment 4 quote
5 put up 6 featured 7 received 8 encouraged
9 female, male 10 stereotypes 11 people of colour 12 minority 13 engineering 14 career
15 gender 16 just about

12 Opposites
1 impossible 2 majority 3 receive 4 female
5 put sth. up

13 Lost words
1 for 2 into 3 on 4 into 5 of 6 on 7 from
8 up 9 in 10 in 11 against 12 in 13 out

14 Odd word out
1 location 2 wage 3 receive 4 few 5 democracy
(Betonung auf der 2. Silbe)

New words p. 47
1 location 2 storyline 3 script 4 rescue
5 identify

15 Plurals
1 giraffe/giraffes 2 thieves 3 national holidays
4 opportunities 5 ostriches 6 wages

16 Word friends
take: ~~choice~~
have: ~~mind~~
be: ~~poverty~~
come: ~~ill~~

New words MORE CHALLENGE p. 52
1° bicycle 2° shameful 3° well heeled 4° draw your attention to 5° instinctively 6° intervened
7° state 8° menacing 9° cursed 10° further
11° Were, about 12° concerned about, welfare
13° motorcycle 14° straight

New words MORE CHALLENGE pp. 52–53
1° concluded 2° If he were to get 3° retreated
4° inexplicable 5° incident 6° has passed
7° account 8° that sort of thing 9° misgivings
10° enriched

17 Find the words
1 curse 2 state 3 welfare 4 bicycle 5 conclude
6 intervene 7 motorcycle

18 Crossword
1 praise 2 mad 3 sweatshop 4 wage
5 → survival 5 ↓ stage 6 siren 7 gingerbread
8 afterwards 9 signature 10 airbrush 11 meme
12 male 13 headlight 14 career 15 → chase
15 ↓ create 16 complete 17 quote 18 burn
19 power 20 politician 21 refugee 22 novel
23 choice 24 → politics 24 ↓ prove 25 interrupt
26 ages 27 lift 28 female 29 via 30 demand

Unit 3: Future visions

New words pp. 54–55
1 vision 2 exoskeleton 3 use 4 firefighter
5 deliver 6 Drones 7 parcel 8 medicine
9 contact lenses 10 power 11 pillow
12 driverless 13 Scientists 14 ahead

1 Definitions
1 firefighter 2 medicine 3 pillow 4 scientist
5 drone

New words p. 56
1 watch 2 touch 3 wearable 4 device
5 Wireless headphones 6 carry 7 board 8 gym
9 data 10 exercise

2 *-less* or *-ful* or *both*?
1 driverless = fahrerlos, führerlos
2 endless = endlos
3 helpless = hilflos; helpful = hilfreich
4 homeless = obdachlos
5 hopeless = hoffnungslos; hopeful = hoffnungsvoll
6 meatless = fleischlos
7 powerless = machtlos; powerful = einflussreich
8 sleepless = schlaflos
9 successful = erfolgreich
10 useless = sinnlos; useful = sinnvoll, hilfreich

New words p. 57
1 buzzed 2 finish 3 groaned 4 head-mounted display

New words pp. 58–59
1 keep on 2 sustainable 3 growth 4 The Middle Ages 5 billion 6 7000 BC 7 1000 AD 8 graph
9 pessimistic 10 optimistic 11 In my view

3 Linking
1 B 2 E 3 G 4 A 5 D 6 F 7 C

New words p. 60
1 frontiers 2 fascinate 3 success 4 Martians
5 planet 6 controversial 7 prediction 8 by 8 pm
9 difficulty/difficulties 10 pioneer 11 would-be
12 signed up for 13 concentrate on

4 What are the words?
1 carrying – wearing
2 exercise – exercises
3 finished – finish

5 Numbers and letters
Hi Grandad,
Thank you for the **parcel** you sent me for my birthday. Had Mum told you that I wanted a **drone**? It's **wonderful**! I can fix my phone to it and take photos **above** the clouds – when they're hanging **low**. Later I can put my phone in my **head-mounted display** and watch things you can't see from the ground. I can hear you **groan**, Grandad ☺. But it's fun and I **spend** a lot of time outside and get a lot of **exercise**. I've always been **fascinated** by new technical gadgets, and I think **drones** can be **useful** in many different **ways**. They can **deliver** things from the **mainland** to small islands or bring **medicine** to people who live in remote areas. When are you coming to see us? I can't **wait to show you all my new photos**.
Love,
Molly

New words p. 61
1 make it 2 suit 3 lovely 4 choir

6 Bits and pieces
1 deliver = (aus)liefern
2 driverless = fahrerlos, führerlos
3 optimistic = optimistisch
4 firefighter = Feuerwehrman/-frau
5 wearable = tragbar
6 exercise = Bewegung, Training
7 device = Gerät, Apparat
8 sustainable = nachhaltig, umweltverträglich; zukunftsfähig
9 pessimistic = pessimistisch
10 success = Erfolg

New words p. 62
1 wishful thinking 2 destination 3 several
4 explore 5 unfortunately

7 What's the right word?
1 wishful thinking 2 choirs 3 signed up 4 was
5 optimistic 6 risen

8 Word labyrinth
unfortunately explore several lovely suit controversial AD prediction growth

Lösungswort: *concentrate*

New words p. 63 and pp. 130–131
1 Global warming 2 caused 3 rise 4 by accident
5 little 6 mainland 7 on our own 8 mob 9 shed
10 graveyard 11 pant(ing)

9 What are the right words: *little – a little – few – a few*?
1 little 2 Few 3 a few 4 a little 5 A few

New words pp. 64–65 and pp. 130–131
1 fear of 2 crowd 3 rowed 4 (just) in case
5 bath 6 backwards 7 It's the way you do it.
8 facing forwards, dizzy 9 blow 10 faint
11 narrator 12 message in a bottle

10 One German word – different English words
1 You/One 2 They/People 3 They/People

11 Opposites
1 finish 2 pessimistic 3 keep on doing sth.
4 backwards 5 less time 6 mainland

New words pp. 63–64
1° deserted 2° derelict 3° burst 4° slow down
5° put off 6° tiny 7° loner 8° hang around
9° whom 10° slipped 11° contain

New words p. 64
1° stormed 2° splashed 3° dragged 4° shore
5° supply 6° paused 7° breath 8° own
9° belongs to 10° we would eat 11° magic
12° sense of 13° beat down 14° replayed
15° nightmare

12 Word snake

	Infinitive	Simple past	Past participle
1	drag	dragged	dragged
2	hang around	hung	hung
3	beat down	beat	beaten
4	rise	rose	risen
5	keep on	kept	kept

13 What are the words: *in, off, on or up*?

1 up 2 off 3 in 4 on

New words p. 66

1 robot 2 exhibition 3 and so on 4 gadget 5 do without 6 drawing

New words pp. 67–69

1 complaint 2 uncomfortable 3 take off 4 battery 5 poor 6 In addition 7 not supposed to 8 count 9 accurate 10 circumstances 11 refund 12 attach 13 receipt 14 within 15 lasted for 16 vague 17 formal 18 thunder

14 Definitions

1 thunder 2 receipt 3 refund 4 accurate 5 count 6 complaint 7 drawing 8 gadget 9 exhibition 10 robot

17 Word search

W	C	O	L	O	U	R	F	U	L	E	L	P	O	E	P
M	I	C	R	A	S	H	E	T	A	G	E	R	G	E	S
U	T	L	U	O	S	T	R	I	C	H	A	X	B	Y	D
L	R	S	D	R	W	A	L	L	E	T	C	Y	T	A	H
T	O	U	R	L	R	E	C	E	I	V	E	I	M	T	C
I	L	C	O	D	I	E	W	E	S	E	R	M	W	C	H
L	L	C	N	A	V	F	N	H	F	O	L	O	G	H	O
I	E	E	E	H	H	E	E	C	N	I	R	D	J	A	I
N	U	S	K	E	G	D	S	I	Y	G	Y	M	E	S	R
G	Q	S	L	A	M	U	M	N	B	O	A	R	D	E	O
U	I	P	T	D	I	Q	R	F	A	C	T	O	R	Y	N
A	N	S	Y	T	I	N	U	T	R	O	P	P	O	S	T
L	U	L	I	F	T	F	R	O	N	T	I	E	R	U	V

New words MORE CHALLENGE p. 74

1° fellow student 2° embarrass 3° humour 4° was robbed 5° class representative 6° gave a speech 7° expression 8° had, done by

16 Crossword

1 use 2 pillow 3 little 4 thunder 5 several 6 fear 7 scientist 8 exercise 9 backwards 10 carry 11 wearable 12 → power 12 ↓ parcel 13 watch 14 rise 15 row 16 bath 17 headphones 18 gym 19 difficulty 20 narrator 21 → graveyard 21 ↓ graph 22 deliver 23 poor 24 device 25 finish 26 explore 27 cause 28 touch 29 suit 30 data 31 sustainable